JOY and HEALING

TORKOM SARAYDARIAN

Aquarian Educational Group
P. O. Box 267
Sedona, Arizona 86336

© 1987 T. Saraydarian

Second Printing 1989

All rights reserved

No part of this publication may be reproduced, stored in a retrieval system, or transmitted in any form, by any means, electronic, mechanical, photocopying, recording or otherwise, without permission in writing from the copyright owner or his representatives.

Library of Congress Number: 87-70416
ISBN: 0-911794-59-X
ISBN: 0-911794-60-3

Printed in the United States of America

Cover Design: Fine Point Graphics
                Sedona, Arizona

Cover Art: "Peafowl"
                Mughal, ca. 1610
                Miniature
                Arthur M. Sackler
                Private Collection

Printed by Delta Lithograph Co., Valencia, California

We would like to express gratitude to the Harvard University Art Museum for the material and permission to reproduce the cover photo.

Contents

A Few Words	i
Joy And Healing — Part I	1
General Observations — Various Appearances Of Joy	18
Exercises On Joy	19
Exercise One	20
Exercise Two	26
Exercise Three	27
Exercise For Creating A New Identity	47
Joy and Healing — Part II	49
How Do We Increase Our Joy?	60
Seven Qualities Of Joy	65
Hindrances To Joy	68
How To Use Joy	71
More Exercises On Joy	81
Meditation On Joy	87
"Joy Is A Special Wisdom"	89
How To Bring Love And Joy To People	93
Joy And The Memory Of Home	109
Love And Joy	125
Index	145

Works by Torkom Saraydarian:

Bhagavad Gita
Challenge for Discipleship
Christ, The Avatar of Sacrificial Love
Cosmic Shocks
Cosmos in Man
A Daily Discipline of Worship
Dialogue with Christ
Fiery Carriage and Drugs
Five Great Mantrams of the New Age
Flame of Beauty, Culture, Love, Joy
Hiawatha and the Great Peace
Hidden Glory of the Inner Man
Hierarchy and the Plan
Irritation—The Destructive Fire
I Was
Joy and Healing
Legend of Shamballa
Psyche and Psychism
Questioning Traveler and Karma
Science of Becoming Oneself
Science of Meditation
Sex, Family and the Woman in Society
Spring of Prosperity
Symphony of the Zodiac
Synthesis
Talks on Agni
Torchbearers
Triangles of Fire
Unusual Court
Woman, Torch of the Future

Aquarian Educational Group
P. O. Box 267
Sedona, Arizona 86336

A
Few Words

Torkom Saraydarian gave two seminars on the subject of joy and its application in our daily life. He also gave a series of exercises on joy, to increase joy in us and release resources of joy latent in us. These exercises are given here.

If you want to do these exercises, we suggest that you do them at your own risk and after obtaining the permission of your psychologist or psychiatrist, in order to be sure that you are not doing something wrong.

At the end of the book we added several chapters from the author's previously published writings on joy, in order to make the reading more beneficial and complete.

The Publishers

Man does not arrive at an understanding of his power without a Guide. Many different traps are hidden on man's path. Each sheltered manifested viper hopes to conceal from man that which is most precious. As a traveler who has lost his way, he does not know in what element to seek success; yet the treasure is within himself.

Aum, para. 371

"We wish that people understand where their panacea lies. We have a holiday when we see that our co-workers have perceived the shield of joy."

M.M.

Joy And Healing
Part I

*D*ue to my good karma, I met many people in my life who were joyful people, who radiated joy in their thinking, emotions, actions, and relationships. Since childhood I have been attracted to joyful people. I have always had a deep desire to know what joy is, what joy can do, and what ways there are to develop joy and be joyful.

Since childhood I have observed that joyful people are magnetic, successful, happy, creative, healthy, and honest. In school I was always around those boys and girls who were joyful. I had a curious feeling that those who did not have joy were either unhealthy, aberrant, or dangerous, and this observation became more convincing as the years passed.

I also observed that joyless students, teachers, and people in general, were like burdens upon my shoulders. They always sapped my energy and enthusiasm. As the years passed, I tried to observe more things related to joy and to increase my information about joy.

For example, I observed the effect of joy on the physical body, the emotions, and thinking. I saw that the absence of joy makes a person lazy and unwilling to strive and labor. The absence of joy makes a person arrogant, insensitive, uncooperative, stubborn, and mentally closed, slow, cunning, or narrow. Most of the joyless people I have seen are sour people and those who use slander, malice, and even treason.

My research was very informal. I did try to record my observations and discoveries, but I always left my papers here and there during my travels. After I had access to libraries, I tried to find books written about the essence, substance, chemistry or anatomy of joy, but I found only superficial remarks. I found neither a book written about joy nor a person who was a specialist on joy. I even met a few psychologists who laughed at me and thought I was a dreamer for being so interested in the psychology of joy.

One of my teachers once said that joy is conditioned by the environment and by the physical and economic well-being of a person. The moment I heard these words, I thought that there was something wrong with them. My further observations revealed that joy is not a result of physical, emotional or mental conditions, but a state of consciousness which surpasses all these conditions and is a conditioning factor or a cause for conditions.

Years passed, and I continued my research. Lately I have read a few books in which joy was mentioned very superficially. After reading these books, I became convinced that the best way to know about joy is to find and observe those people who have joy.

One of the most joyful people I met in my life was my father. He was a born optimist. He was healthy, good-looking, energetic, and full of enthusiasm and striving. He was an incessant worker. My father passed through the darkest hours that anyone could pass through. All his relatives — eighty-seven people — were butchered by the Turks. He was spared with my mother because he was a pharmacist and the hospital in our town did not have a pharmacist.

Years passed, and after the war and the genocide were over, my father moved our family to a big city where he thought life would be safer. He opened a very modern pharmacy there. In a few years' time, the pharmacy was known all over the city for its prompt and good service.

One summer morning, two policemen came and informed my father that they had an order from the government to close the doors of the pharmacy for a week. According to his usual manner, my father invited them into his office, offered them tea and cake, and wanted to know the reason why. They said that another pharmacy which belonged to an Armenian had poisoned an officer. The pharmacist was under investigation, and until the investigation was over, all Armenian pharmacies would be closed.

My father took the news very calmly. He waited to see how they put wax seals on the locks of his pharmacy. Then he gave a very strange smile and took a taxi to go home. His smile was a condensation of many thoughts — difficult to express in words. In his smile there were foresight, insight, and prophecy. He knew what was going to happen, and he had already decided not to be crumbled in the hands of fate. His smile was clearly saying that no matter what happened, he would be above it.

On the way home, he was very calm and he was smiling in serenity. Mother was surprised that we were home early. "What is the matter?" she asked.

I was waiting for Daddy to condemn and curse the situation, but he smiled at Mother and said, "It's nothing serious. We have been instructed to take a fifteen-day leave until the government finishes some investigations about a pharmacy which is suspected of having prepared a poisonous prescription ... or something like that...."

"What action are we going to take?" she asked.

"Just be patient, and all will go the way it should."

Then he took Mother and me to dinner on an island which was covered with pine trees. The fragrance of pine, the dinner, and the joyful environment brought cheer to our hearts.

During the next few days, my father made an effort to reopen his pharmacy by trying to call the president of the government, Ataturk himself. Ataturk was an old friend of my father who used to visit our pharmacy. I had seen them conversing a few times before that. I remember one particular conversation they had had several years earlier. As the conversation was going on, Ataturk suddenly looked at my father and said, "Yervant, do you love your own nation, your country?"

"Yes, sir," said my father. "I love my country — Armenia."

Ataturk smiled a strange smile and said, "I am proud of you. Whoever loves his own can love the country in which he is living. You are a trustful and fearless man, and I am proud of you."

And he shook my father's hand and went to his car with his guards. Then he came back from the car and gave my father one of his pencils.

My father had hoped that now Ataturk would clear all the doubts about the pharmacy in one second, and he could reopen the pharmacy. But it was impossible to reach him. All my father's efforts were blocked.

Six months passed, and early one morning a policeman came and gave my father the key to his pharmacy, and a note from the government which said, "The case is closed. We wish you success."

My father smiled. He knew their language well. He took a few dollars from his pocket and gave them to the waiting policeman. "Here, you may use these few dollars," he said. "Thank you for the key." And he smiled the same smile that he had smiled when they were sealing the doors of the pharmacy. The policeman disappeared without saying thank you.

On the way to the pharmacy, my father said, "For me, all life seems like a play. It is not real. That is why sometimes loss or gain does not make a difference to the actors.... Does it?"

"I guess not."

"If we lose, we can make it again. If we make it again, we may lose it again.... Well, let's see how the pharmacy did in my absence."

We unlocked the door, and Father slowly and carefully opened it. The whole pharmacy was empty. Father took a long breath and began to laugh.

I was scared.

He continued laughing. Then he said, "I bet you that the safe will also be empty."

The safe was empty. All our cash, jewelry, and gold were gone. Daddy looked at the key, threw it away and said, "I knew exactly how things were going to be. Let's get out of here and go eat a good lunch."

At the restaurant people congratulated him on reopening the pharmacy. "Thank you, thank you," he said. "We are going to start from scratch." And he began to laugh.

"Daddy," I said, "why do you laugh?"

"For the first time I feel great, so great about this," he said. "Such tragedies cannot take away the joy of my heart. This is a great challenge for me to prove to my Lord that I can start my service again."

At night, many doctors, psychiatrists and other professional friends came to comfort him and encourage him. He served wine, made jokes, and made people laugh. And he said, "I am, in a sense, glad, because a heavy load has been taken from my shoulders, but I am sorry for those whom I was serving almost free." One of my father's habits was to give poor people their prescriptions free.

Years later, once when we were talking about this incident, he said, "We saved energy, health and money by not falling into depression, anger, hatred, and irritation, but by maintaining our joy, patience, and serenity. If we had lost these three diamonds, the future would have been lost for us." Then with the same strange smile he said, "Darkness also needs his share."

Once when I was six years old, I saw a butterfly while I was in a field with my father. It was so big and beautiful that I wanted to see it more closely. I think the butterfly knew my feelings because as I ran after it in great joy, it would light on a certain branch or flower for a few seconds to give me a chance to see it more closely, and then fly away.

As I ran after it, the butterfly again gave me a chance to go closer to it, but this time at a greater distance. After a while I looked back and I was almost two miles away from my father who, I guessed, was happy for my joy.

Eventually the butterfly stopped on a bush, opened its wings, and let me come very close to it and observe its beauty. On its wings it had the colors of the rainbow, running in stripes in the shape of a leaf. I was in extreme joy, to such a degree that I started to run around and around the bush, dancing and singing a self-made song:

> "Butterfly, butterfly,
> I love you.
> I love your coat.
> I love your colors.
> Thank you
> for sharing your beauty
> with me."

It was almost sunset when I came back to the tree under which my father was sitting. "Did you like the butterfly?" he asked.

Instead of answering him, I began to dance and sing my self-made song. He embraced me and threw me on his back, and we walked a few miles in silence. Then he sang the words of my song with a new tune.

"Did you like the song?" he asked.

"Yes."

"Do you see? Joy creates songs and beauty. It creates poems ... and this is your first poem...."

At night in my sleep, I was still with the beautiful butterfly. The next morning I went to my father's bed very early and said, "Do you know what?"

"What?"

"I did not touch the butterfly because I was afraid I would hurt it."

He looked at me and a pearl of a tear jumped out of his right eye and fell down over his nose. Then, pulling me into his bed, we slept together for a few hours. This was one of my diary leaves of joy.

I had some teachers who were people of great joy. Some of them were hermits who were living in a state of continuous ecstasy. Others were principals or deans of great institutions. One particular teacher was so powerful in his joy that he used to fill our hearts with joy when he entered our classroom, or when he appeared in a crowded hall.

Another teacher was full of joy all day for all sorts of reasons. For example, he was joyful because of the singing birds, the flowers, the trees, the streams.... Children used to fill him with great joy, or evoke joy from him. I never saw him angry or irritated. In the most complicated and frightening situations he used to express great joy and wisdom. He passed away in his sleep at age one hundred and seventeen, with a beautiful smile on his face....

When I was a teenager, I wondered what kind of joy to have — the joy of hermits or the joy of warriors of life? I came out of the last monastery I visited in 1939 and dedicated myself to the Teaching. The greatest challenge in my life is still to have joy in spreading the Teaching of joy in trying conditions. The following pages will explain my feelings about the miracle of joy.

1. **Joy is a state of beingness in which your consciousness is not conditioned by the environment or by the thoughts, emotions, and activities going on in your environment.** The roar of life is heard, but it does not affect your consciousness. A moment of joy is a moment of an unconditioned state of consciousness. You have joy, not because things and conditions are right or wrong, but because joy flows down from your Core into your vehicles.

2. **Joy is a state of beingness in which no one and nothing can limit your love and sense of unity.** This is a moment of abstraction. The Core of man is bliss. In striving to be your True Self and coming closer to your True Self, you release greater bliss. All that we search for in this world is bliss.

As we detach from the problems of our threefold personality vehicles and withdraw into higher states of consciousness, we feel greater joy and greater bliss. The difference between bliss and joy is easy to find. Joy is bliss sensed and experienced in the higher emotional and mental planes. Bliss is experienced only in the Spiritual Triad and on higher planes.

8 Joy And Healing — Part I

Any moment the ray of bliss is trapped or experienced in the personality vehicles or in your soul, you feel joy. Outer life, things, people, and conditions do not give you joy, but they may evoke joy or call it out from your Core. For example, beauty, goodness, righteousness and freedom can evoke joy.

Bliss is like a ray of light which is part of your True Self. It pours out from your Self if the right conditions are created or if it is evoked by the right conditions. But once the flow of joy is established, no condition and nothing can stop its radiation.

The depository of joy consists of our Inner Watch, the human soul, and the Spiritual Triad. If these centers are contacted by our consciousness, the flow of joy starts and increases. When a person communicates with his soul, he feels the joy existing in the human heart. When he contacts his Inner Watch, he feels the joy of the Great Ones. When he contacts the Spiritual Triad, the joy of the Leader of this planet pours into his heart. We are told that greater areas of joy exist in Space ... but they are far from our reach at present.

The more you are your True Self, the more joy you have. The more you are controlled by your threefold personality vehicles and identified with their problems, the less joy and the more pain you have.

Bliss is achieved through contemplation, samadhi, ecstasy, and withdrawal into higher levels of awareness. Those who learn meditation and eventually do contemplation can gradually touch the spheres of bliss and charge their lives with deep joy.

There was a Teacher who once entered into samadhi — deep contemplation — while his disciples were sitting around him. Suddenly an arrow flew and pierced his shoulder. The disciples did not know what to do, but they thought that if he had not been affected, they should not bring him back to consciousness until he himself came back.

After the Teacher came back to his consciousness, he inquired about the arrow. "Master," they said, "one of your enemies shot this arrow at you. Let us take it out." Then with a certain type of surgery they took the arrow out of his arm.

Joy And Healing — Part I

The further you go out of your physical body, the less you sense it. The deeper you go into your Self, the greater is your joy, the more inclusive is your love, and your mind operates in the vision of unity and synthesis. The further you are from your True Self, the more separative you are in your thoughts, emotions and actions.

Joy usually comes to your personality like a pleasant shock, and disappears. But if you give yourself time to experience joy and if you let it flow as long as possible, you may have a chance to observe what joy does for you, for your bodies, and for your environment.

People drink a cup of wine or do other pleasant things in such a hurry that they do not taste them or observe them. Also, there are many factors in you and in your environment which are ready to put out your flaming charcoal or pour cold water on your joy and encapsulate it in your aura. Hundreds of such capsules are floating in your aura. These capsules contain a great amount of joy energy, which can be used for upliftment, healing, labor, and sacrificial service.

You see a flower and feel joy and you say, "It is really beautiful." And then you turn your face away to do something else. But if you look longer and see the form of the petals and the colors of the flower, if you sense its fragrance ... you may have a chance at the same time to experience the effect of joy on you.

There are two kinds of observation: observation identified with the personality, and observation identified with the flow of joy. We have so much joy in our natures, but we do not enjoy it because we are in a hurry. Any joy that is not assimilated or enjoyed, any joy that is hit by certain thoughts or attacked by the environment or certain persons, crystallizes and turns into a blockage in our auras. When such blockages increase, we avoid everything that may evoke joy from our Core.

Joy must be an active flow, or a circulatory wave in your aura. Such a wave is a cause of health, happiness, energy, optimism, and enthusiasm. But if joy is blocked and crystallized, it may cause you various troubles. For example, sadness, grief, and depression are often the result of blocked or imprisoned joy in your system.

I know a girl who fell into a deep depression and apathy for years when suddenly her boyfriend was killed in Vietnam. Psychologists have many different ways of analyzing such events, but in reality, when joy is frozen it often freezes the heart and the consciousness, too. Of course, there are measures you can take to fight against the moments when your joy is "taken away" from you.

When you are in joy, hang on to it, taste it, inhale it, and try to make it flow into your aura and nerves by the power of your consciousness, as if you were guiding the flow of water into the trenches of your garden.

I saw a man watching the sunset. He was all joy. He was in worship. He was the rays of the sun. He was the symphony of the forms of colors.... I saw him stand motionless for another thirty minutes after the sun had disappeared.

I saw one of my Teachers watching a huge blooming tree with tears in his eyes.

I saw a friend of mine in ecstasy during the recitation of a poem.

Once my mother was gone in her consciousness for one hour after she listened to some flute music.

When you experience joy, try to continue your feeling for at least a few hours, staying on the wave of the joy. One minute of joy can turn on all the lights in you and make you a more successful, beautiful and attractive person, even for many months.

Some people eat like dogs. They do not chew their food at all, but swallow it very fast. If they would chew their food, they would have the joy of tasting the food. They would have a chance to assimilate the food and use it for their well-being.

This is the same for everything we want to enjoy. Take your time, do not hurry.... The moment of joy is a sacred moment for transformation.

3. **Joy is a state of beingness in which you energize in your environment all that is beautiful, good, and righteous.** Joy increases all that is beautiful in life. Joy encourages people who are working for the transformation of humanity, or who are trying to alleviate pain and suffering in the world.

Every time you are in the presence of a joyful person, you feel the kindling of your creative fires. You feel the strengthening of the power of your striving toward perfection. You feel enthusiasm in your labor and a purpose in your life. All these gifts come from above, from the source of joy, through joy. But if you are joyless or sour, hateful or angry, you nourish evil, crime and hatred in others. It is very interesting that the thorns of life cannot survive in an atmosphere of real joy.

The more joy you give, the more you increase goodness, creativity and nobility in the world. Most criminals, prisoners and insane people come from homes which were full with grief, irritation, anger, hatred, greed and vanity. Be joyful in the presence or in the company of your spouse and children, and you will increase the potentials for their success and survival.

Joyfulness makes people love you, as your joy is the nourishment of their souls. If you teach people with joy, they will understand your teaching, they will remember your teaching, and they will try to live according to your teaching.

When you impose your will with hatred, irritation, and anger, you make people obey you for a while, but once they are free from your pressure, they will be your worst enemies. Even your children will rebel against you and at a very unexpected moment abandon you.

Real joy fertilizes and nourishes the garden of your heart and the field of labor of your life.

4. **Joy is a state of beingness in which you attract forces of inspiration, abundance, harmony, and vitality.** Joy creates a special chemistry in your aura and in your mental, astral, and etheric bodies, which become magnetic to the currents of higher inspirations coming from your Soul, from your Teachers, and from

higher sources or centers of wisdom. Also, such a magnetic atmosphere enables you to translate the currents of inspiration correctly and creatively.

The forces of abundance are those forces which make things flow toward your direction. A joyful person sees how books, money, land, and many other objects that he needs flow toward his direction, because the forces of abundance know that he will use them for the Common Good, as a service for humanity.

Abundance and joy are closely related to each other. A joyful person enjoys the things he has, but for a joyless person all his possessions are like his prison. They are the source of his unhappiness or — worst of all — the cause of his spiritual and moral destruction.

Joy attracts forces of harmony. People cooperate voluntarily with a joyful person. The forces of harmony bring him not only a healthy body, but harmonious emotions, harmonious thoughts, harmonious plans and goals.... They create conditions in which his life is harmonious with the rhythm of his Soul, of his nation, and of humanity. A joyful person never thinks, feels, speaks, or acts in a way that is not harmonious with the highest aspirations of humanity.

Joy awakens in you a buried sense, whose echo is the ability of your ears to recognize harmony in sound. But when this buried sense is awakened, you fit into the symphony of life and you live a life of harmony.

Joy brings vitality, not only to your body, but also to your thoughts, emotions, actions, and expressions. You become full of vitality; you become a source of vitality in your environment. You transmit energies that nourish, uplift, cure, and strengthen people around you. Even trees, bushes, flowers, and animals feel and enjoy your vitality. Joy is the source of vitality and the main cause of the strength of your immune system.

5. Joy is a state of beingness in which you expand your consciousness toward higher and lower kingdoms and establish constructive and creative communications with them. Your consciousness cannot expand in a gloomy state of mind. It is possible for a person to gather knowledge, learn formulas, or build plans while his consciousness remains the same.

There is a great difference between the consciousness and the mind. The mind can grow at the expense of the consciousness, but use all its tools against its own survival. When the consciousness expands, a person can think from cause to effect and from effect to cause. He thinks inclusively, from all possible viewpoints, having in his mind the good of all.

The mind can turn into a separative tool, which works for one group but against another group. The consciousness does not work for separative interests. An expanding consciousness does not allow the mind to work for one kingdom and neglect the rest. The expanding consciousness knows that all various kingdoms are part of a great whole. It does not mobilize one group against another group.

A person with an expanded consciousness has a field of action which is above and below, below and above, as parts of one reality. His relationship with higher kingdoms is as creative as his relationship with lower kingdoms. His creativity is a labor to create more harmonious relationships between them and open possibilities for the lives of lower kingdoms to advance into higher kingdoms.

6. **Joy is a state of beingness in which no feeling of separatism, no thought to create cleavages, and no awareness of loneliness exist.** Real joy annihilates all separatism, cleavages, and loneliness. Separatism is the result of an unhappy soul. An unhappy and joyless person lives far away from his own Core, which is the central point of unity and synthesis. Being far away from his Home, he wanders in the valleys of loneliness, cleavage and separatism. He thinks, speaks and works for his separative interests. In order to keep his separative interests alive, he creates cleavages in those who are against his interests. Eventually people recognize his motives, learn his tricks, and see his plans — and they slowly withdraw from his presence and leave him alone to continue worshipping himself at the expense of others.

A lonely and joyless person eventually loses all that he has accumulated, and lives a miserable life. A joyful person radiates forces of unity and he never feels lonely. He never commits the crime of creating cleavages; he never separates people. He has many friends who are ready to give their lives for him because they feel that joy is the real message of oneness, unity, and synthesis. You feel all this in a moment of joy when your beingness is elevated, but in the next moment the clouds of your doubts, self-interest, greed, and jealousy cover the rays of your joy and you fall again into the darkness of your habits, prejudices, superstitions and vanities.

7. Joy is a state of beingness in which you feel that you are one with the One Self manifesting in all various forms of life in the Universe. You feel that your creative powers are in no way limited, but that they are capable of making you reach the stars.

Joy makes you feel that you are the Universe, that you are part of the Almighty Creative Power. In joy you feel that you are not limited in the present stage of your achievement, but that you are capable of unfolding, expanding, and reaching perfection "as your Father in heaven is perfect."

The path leading man to God is the path of joy. It is because of the presence of an infinite joy in their hearts that all martyrs of humanity consciously and voluntarily sacrificed their lives to help humanity, while the gophers of humanity occupied themselves with eating the roots of the tree of humanity.

8. Joy is a state of beingness in which you develop patience, perseverance, endurance, and changelessness of spirit. Where there is real joy, there will be no fluctuations.

Patience cannot endure without joy. Patience without joy burns all your centers and creates irritation. Joy is patient.

Perseverance is the result of joy. Joy keeps your spirit vital and your path clear. Perseverance with joy is a bonfire on a cold day in the desert. Perseverance with joy is an arrow flying to the target. Perseverance with joy is a process of transformation of yourself into the image you hold in your vision.

Endurance is pain and suffering, if it is not inspired by joy. Joy makes you endure hardships and trying conditions. Joy proves to you that you can do and you can be. Joy galvanizes your vehicles in such a degree that they can resist any attack and endure labor and pressure until you reach your goal.

Joy gives you a taste of changelessness. The Changeless One is the bliss within you. In joyful moments, you experience a timelessness, spacelessness, and changelessness. It may be one second of joy, but what a glory is contained in that moment of joy, if your eyes and ears were fast enough to record the richness and magnitude of the beauty contained in that moment.

Fluctuations are the signs of an unhappy person. Those who have not yet touched the fire of joy are unhappy persons. An unhappy person is directionless. Every time he changes his direction, he thinks that the new direction is not the one he wants to follow. He not only changes his directions and goals, but, worst of all, he fluctuates between them.

On the other hand, for a joyful person, any direction leading to beauty, goodness, righteousness, joy and freedom is part of the same one direction, because of the joy that makes all various directions lead to the Source of joy.

9. Joy is a state of beingness in which you develop an increasing sense of responsibility, a sense of righteousness, and a sense of practical involvement with life in general. The sense of responsibility turns into a heavy load on your back and a source of resentment if it is not the result of real joy. Joy brings the sense of responsibility into existence. Joy develops it and makes it an instrument of great service.

The sense of righteousness is the fruit of joy. Righteousness without joy turns into terror, and eventually creates a tyrant, a self-righteous person who uses his power of righteousness to destroy people before they grow and give flowers. The sense of righteousness is a very advanced sense which makes a person see how the seed is in the process of growing and blooming.

Righteousness is the ability to hold the flower in the mind and encourage the seed to achieve perfection. Only in joy is righteousness understood.

Joy does not take you into deserts, but it makes you work and live in a world of problems, difficulties and dangers. It makes you become involved with the labor going on for the redemption of humanity. Joy pulls you toward your duty and makes you work wherever possible to distribute joy, just as you would distribute food to the hungry and water to the thirsty.

10. Joy is a state of beingness in which your Treasury opens Its doors, and hidden talents, precious memories, and past wisdom and attainments flow into your conscious mind.

Joy is released gradually, and it slowly opens the doors of your Treasury, your Chalice. Out of your Treasury pour down talents which you developed and later treasured in order to develop other talents. Out of your Treasury pour down precious memories which you can use now to build your mansions of light. Out of your Treasury pours down past wisdom which now comes in handy in the labor you are engaged in. Thus you find yourself surrounded with the treasures of your past, and with them you serve in greater and higher fields, with the same benevolent purpose.

If you can stay long in your joy, you will be able to see how many jewels that were lost in past lives fall in front of your feet in the time of great need. Life accumulates all your diamonds in order to give them back to you at the moments when you can use them constructively, without self-interest, but for the good of all living beings. Joy is a key to many greater treasuries.

11. Joy is a state of beingness in which your physical, emotional and mental natures go through a process of integration and alignment. Joy is the "communication fluid" between the parts of the one "engine." Through joy, your physical, emotional and mental natures work as a unit. Then this unit is aligned with the awareness unit, the human soul. Thus as integration and alignment continue, a great amount of joy is registered and used.

Integrated and aligned human beings never try to cause pain and suffering to other people. Those who hurt people do not need lectures or psychoanalysis, but integration and alignment through joy.

Joy is not considered a healing factor in psychological and psychiatric treatments at this time, but very soon it will be accepted and the potentials of joy will be used to wipe out the ills of humanity. This is not a prophecy of doom, but a prophecy of joy.

12. Joy is a state of beingness in which all evil currents in you are arrested, all attacks of dark forces are repulsed, a shield is built around you, and the Watchman in you is alert. I leave this definition to the reader to work with as best he can.

We all have many moments of joy in our lives, but they have been buried by pain and suffering. We must try to reach them, find them, and bring them to the surface. There are no big and small joys; all joys are the same joy, but the intensity of feeling and the depth of registration differ.

General Observations — Various Appearances Of Joy

1. Radiance in eyes and face
2. Sharp thinking
3. Alertness and sensitiveness
4. Vitality
5. Punctuality
6. Health
7. Lovingness
8. Diligence
9. Openness and freedom
10. Cooperativeness

The energy of joy is:

- Regenerating
- Purifying
- Dispersing
- Expanding
- Linking
- Unfolding
- Harmonizing

Joy is the energy of transmutation, transformation, and transfiguration.

Exercises On Joy

*A*s a foundation for the following exercises, let us remember that every true experience of joy which was locked in our auras in the past can be released through such exercises and the flow of joy energy can be used to uplift ourselves, to create integration, alignment, and harmony, and even to eliminate many disturbances in our natures.

Many people who have tried these exercises have written to me to say that they feel like new persons. My wish is that some psychologists and psychiatrists take interest in these exercises and use them for the advantage of those who knock on their doors for help.

Exercise One

Close your eyes. Relax.

Try to remember a joy that you experienced in the earliest part of your life. Go back in your mind and try to find a moment of joy as early as possible in your life. At this stage, just remember the experience.

Try to remember where it occurred, when it occurred, and how it occurred. Remember the time it occurred and the weather that day. Remember the environment you were in when it occurred, what you were wearing, and how you looked. Try to remember those who were with you in that moment.

This phase is very important. Go very slowly until everything is clear in your memory.

After this is done properly, try to re-experience your joy, as if it is happening at this very moment. Try to feel the joy through all your nature.

Do this at least three times, until your memory is clear and your experience of joy is real. Do not listen to your analytical mind. Do not listen to your other memories. Just enjoy the joy and feel it as a little child does.

It is possible that you will cry. Let your tears flow, but continue experiencing your joy as you experienced it in the past. Be the age you were when you experienced the joy.

Now try again to experience your joy, but this time let your past being enjoy the experience, and in the meantime, you observe what is happening to that person who is re-experiencing his past joy. Observe what is happening to his mind, emotions, and body. Observe the effect of his joy on others and on the environment.

Go very slowly and try to be clear in your observation. Let this take from half an hour to two hours. If you feel comfortable and have the time, you can do it for two hours daily. You may consider the following rules:

1. Ask the permission of your psychiatrist or doctor before doing this exercise.
2. Do not do this exercise within two hours of eating.
3. Do not do this exercise after 10:00 p.m.
4. Do not do this exercise within six hours after having sexual relations.
5. Do not do this exercise if you are tired or exhausted. First rest.
6. Do not hurry in re-experiencing your past joy.
7. You can work on one experience three times, on three different occasions in a week. Then remember another experience of joy and repeat the exercise. After every exercise, end your session by visualizing a white light surrounding your body and penetrating every part of your body. This may deepen your calmness and serenity.
8. At the end of your session, always wait a few minutes before you open your eyes. During these few minutes, touch your body and remember where you are. Try to hear some noises outside. Then open your eyes.
9. After you go over seven experiences, take a rest for fifteen days and try to be joyful in your daily life as much as you can.
10. The exercises of re-experiencing joy must last for six months. Then you may start a new exercise for another six months. The new exercise should be done following exactly the same rules.

It is also very important not to compare your past with your present. For example, when you are experiencing a joy of seeing your teacher and experiencing his presence when you were ten years old, try to really enjoy that moment. Do not let your mind go off the track and tell you that the teacher has since died in an accident or that you lost him when you moved to another country.... If you are enjoying a flower, enjoy it with your totality and do not let your mind, through association, deliver you a message of a memory in which you presented the same flower to someone who rejected you. Total absorption into your joy experiences is imperative if you want to release the accumulated energy of joy into your system.

It is also possible that your joy is overwhelming and floods your system, but then suddenly a thought comes and tells you: "This happened in the past, and you cannot have such a joy again in your life." Refuse to listen to such a thought by gradually merging more deeply into your experience. Remember that there is no limitation for a free soul and that joy can be experienced in progressively greater quality and depth.

Remember that an experience of joy is a process of putting money in your savings account. Your greater achievements in the future will be the result of the accumulated joy which you take out of the bank and use to achieve your dreams. These exercises are the steps of going to the bank and releasing your money, with interest.

The ancients used to call a person's Treasury a well in which you drop your joy, and it disappears from your sight. This joy must be pulled out and used. When you do this exercise in the right way, you will start witnessing all the blessings mentioned on previous pages.

Remember also that joy can be experienced physically, emotionally, mentally, and spiritually — separately or all together. Joy must be felt physically, emotionally, mentally, and spiritually. First you will have difficulty discerning between the levels of the feeling of joy, but gradually you will see that there are differences between joys experienced on various levels.

Often we think about joy as if it were a feeling. The reality is that joy is a substance, an electrical and fiery substance, which will be possible to measure in the future, when we find the time to stand above our stupidities. Joy flows through the nerve channels, muscles, bones, and bloodstream, as electricity flows through wires. Joy gives light, heat, and coolness, and puts great plans into action, as electricity produces light, heat, and moves mighty factories. But one must develop pure observation to see or feel the substance of joy.

In your exercises, remember that joy is a substance, a fiery flow of energy.... And remember that it radiates out from your own Core.

One day a young boy came to my office with tears in his eyes and said, "Please help me. It is very embarrassing to me and my family when the police catch me while I am drunk or doped. I really want to give up alcohol, marijuana and other drugs, but I have no will power...."

I advised him to go to professional people for help, but he kept coming back to me again and again, saying, "I know you can cure me!" After observing him and thinking about him, I suddenly realized that he was trying to find joy in his life. He was thinking that drugs, marijuana and alcohol could lead him to joy. Joy was his hidden motive, his hidden goal.

Immediately I called him and told him that I could help him, if he came to see me two hours daily for seven days. He agreed to come. What I did was very simple. I made him sit relaxed, go back in his imagination to his childhood, and start finding points or experiences of joy. I made him experience these joys again and again, until all the events were clear, complete and real in his consciousness.

After doing the exercises for ten days, the change in the boy began to appear. He was free from the control of his vices and radiated joy and peace. I have never since seen him using any drugs, marijuana or alcohol. Once when I asked him how he was doing, he answered, "I was looking for my joy in the wrong places, but now I found it. I do not need artificial things to make me happy; I am already happy."

When most people find real joy in their hearts, they resign from all of those artificial things which make them miserable. People aspire to bliss, to joy, and to being one with their Self. Finding the experiences of joy and bringing them to the surface of their present level of consciousness will give people enough joy and enough strength not to be trapped by artificial methods.

Try to give joy, and you will save people. Christ said, "My joy I give to you."

Most people use drugs and fall into various vices because they are unhappy, because they are disillusioned by their parents, because their vision and striving are destroyed, or because they do not see any future and hope for themselves. Joy will fill the vacuum of their hearts. It will make them re-experience their past joys and experience the joys of others. It will make them create joyful moments in their lives....

The use of joy must be practiced daily. Be joyful, and then transfer the current of joy to your children every morning and every night. Transfer the current of your joy to the meals you prepare, to the objects you use, to the clothes you wear, to the water you drink, to the office, to others.... Let joy circulate in everything you touch.

Before you read your lessons, feel joy. Before you open your door to go out in the morning, feel joy. Before you turn on the ignition of your car, feel joy. Do not start or end anything without first feeling joy. Joyful people are the carriers and distributors of the spirit of God.

People ask if one can bring joy with him from previous lives. In reality, there are no previous or future lives; there is only one life and one Monad, living one life. For the living one, there is no time and location; there is only one beam of light with many beads on it.

Joy is the beam of light giving life and beauty to each bead. As the beam of light is a unit, so are the beads, separate in time but one in essence, as each future bead is the result of the previous bead. The future condition of each bead is the result of the relationship between the light of the beam and the bead.

Joy is a contact between the beads and the beam of light. The deeper is the contact, the greater is the joy. These exercises are an effort to keep joy flowing into the beads and to thus make the beads in greater harmony with the living beam. At present, the consciousness of man is identified with the beads. That is why there are many beads for him. As he identifies his consciousness with the beam of light, he will realize that there is only one life lived in many beads, and that is him.

Joy can be used in factories, in big corporations, and in various associations, to increase the potentials of employees or workers. Joy can be used in government agencies and in political parties to expand their horizons, adjust their sense of values, and deepen their insight and foresight. Joy can be used by physicians, surgeons, and even psychiatrists.

I knew a heart surgeon who began to develop a very negative attitude toward his wife and children. One day he told me that he was having difficulty with the hospital administration, and he was afraid that troubles were accumulating over his head. After he finished talking, I proposed to him that he start some exercises with me. His first question was whether the exercises were valid, whether they were approved by medical doctors or Ph.D.'s. I told him that he was the only one who needed to approve the exercises, after seeing the results of the exercises.

He postponed working with me ... but when he saw later that his condition at the hospital and at his home was becoming worse and worse, he came to my home and said, "Do those damned exercises, if you can help me."

We spent the first session making him learn to smile, and I explained to him the mystery of the smile. At the end of the session he was quite happy.

I worked with this man for six months. He not only regained his reputation, but he was also promoted in the hospital administration and he became the one to whom many people looked for help. Once his wife said to me, "I do not know what happened to me. I was planning to divorce him, but now I have fallen in love with him again."

Our social conditions can change as a whole if we prepare fields of joy and plant seeds of joy, instead of attacking each other, threatening each other, imposing our authority, and cultivating fear and hypocrisy.

Exercise Two

This exercise is different from the former one. In this exercise, instead of remembering your own joy and re-experiencing it, you are going to remember an event in which you witnessed some other person who was really in joy, and try to feel, understand, and re-experience his joy. Do not forget the rules given for the first exercise.

First remember the occasion. See the person as he was. See yourself as you were, and remember the time, the weather, the persons involved, and the one who was really in joy.

Try, first of all, to observe the way he was joyful — physically, emotionally, and mentally. Remember in detail his manners, his voice, and his words.

After you do this several times in one session, try to share his joy. Do not be him, but share his joy. When you are really able to share his joy many times, each time with greater details from your memory, try to observe how his joy was transferred into you and why.

Do this exercise for six months, three times weekly. Each week try to find a new person who was in joy for various reasons and share his joy.

Exercise Three

The third exercise is the reverse of the second one. Remember an event in which a person shared your joy. Do this as many times as you wish, and then try to observe how and why your joy was deeply felt and experienced by him. Repeat this whole exercise for six months.

Remember that to release joy is more precious than anything you do in the world, because joy will condition your success, your health, and your right relationships with others; it will brighten your intellect, strengthen your heart, and destroy the assaults of darkness.

The exercises on joy can be carried on further for the greater benefit of you and of those with whom you are related. For example, after you have released as many joy capsules within your memory as possible, you can relax and visualize an event in the future which gives you an extraordinary measure of joy. This should not be an event which you wish for or expect to happen, but an event which you see going on exactly as you visualize it.

Think what can make you really joyful. Start with a visualized event. Use your creative imagination, and for three sessions try to do it each time with more details and finding a deeper and more valuable joy. You may start with physical or material things, and then go to emotional events, then to mental events, then to spiritual events. You may transcend time and space through your creative imagination, travel in space to the stars, and imagine a new life or new events there.

See how your creative imagination can transcend all familiar concepts and cliché formations of life. You can create a life in higher dimensions which is unlike the life going on upon this planet.

Do not have any limitation in creating events of joy through your visualization. Try to enjoy them in all your vehicles, in the deepest degree that you can.

Do this for six months, and record the results and effects on your life and on the lives of others.

Creative imagination can prepare your soul to take giant steps in the future, building some kind of ladder on the path of future achievements through these exercises. The more your thoughts are occupied with images of joy, the greater will be your striving toward the future.

Exercises on joy never end, and they should not end. You can also add the following to the list of your exercises:

1. Remember those joys that you intentionally caused to others. Work in detail.

2. Remember joys that others intentionally caused to you. Remember them in detail.

3. Remember the moments of joy you received from Nature. Re-experience these kinds of joy again and again — the joy that you received from flowers, fields, meadows, rivers, waterfalls, forests, certain trees, rainbows, sunsets and sunrises, birds.... You have thousands of such joys. Release them, and energize your whole nature with joy. Try to live in joy.

In doing the above exercises, try to remember the specific events in detail, if possible. Do not jump from one event to the other. Take your time.

Once I tried such exercises with my students in school, and the results were overwhelming. The students' grades, as well as their relationships with each other, improved tremendously. The whole school improved as if a miracle had happened. I especially worked on the problem children, and their anger, remorse, hatred, and roughness gradually disappeared.

Joy is a miracle; it creates miraculous changes within our psyche. The greatest benefactors of humanity are those who bring more joy to humanity. The greatest benefactors of humanity are those who create those conditions in which people enjoy more the miracle of life.

Do not believe those who, in the name of future prosperity, health and happiness, spread sorrow, grief, pain, limitations, and slavery. They are aberrant people, and they need to heal themselves with joy.

"Joy is a special wisdom," said a great sage once. Through joy you can solve problems. You do not need to punish people. Make them understand why they were wrong through exercises of joy, and they will gather wisdom. Punishing people creates more misery than you can imagine. We must not try to solve problems through wars. It has never worked yet, and it will never work. The problems of the world must be solved by training the leaders of the world with joy.

A person must never be promoted into a high position if he has no joy. Joy is more important than a person's I.Q. Sad, negative, pessimistic people, people who feel happy exploiting others, people who feel happy seeing tears in the eyes of others, cannot be leaders. Leaders must be trained from childhood, and they must be transformed in the stream of joy. Then we will have great leaders who can solve problems and lead humanity to the age of happiness, joy and bliss.

Unhappiness is a very contagious disease. Those who fall into unhappiness are those who break the laws of love, unity and service. We must try to heal through the medicine of joy. It will take time, but we will eventually do it.

Remember that hilarity has nothing to do with joy. Hilarity is a disease. "The pursuit of happiness" must be understood correctly. The pursuit of happiness is not a process of being happy at the expense of others. The pursuit of happiness is an intelligent way of living to bring happiness to the entire humanity, to animals, plants, birds, and all of Nature.

The pursuit of happiness is not license of sex, drugs, crimes and exploitation. The pursuit of happiness is a process of healthy living, healthy aspiration and clear thinking. It is a life lived in "harmlessness, self-forgetfulness, and right speech."

The pursuit of happiness is the pursuit of freedom — freedom from want, freedom from fear, freedom of religion, freedom of right speech. There is no happiness unless the human essence is capable of being free from all conditions which prevent him from being beautiful, full of goodness, righteous and joyful.

To turn the tide of the contemporary flow of negativity, imposition, exploitation, greed and totalitarianism, which are the sources of human unhappiness, we must reconstruct our psychology and start being like little children who can solve very complicated problems by surrendering themselves to the wings of joy. A child generally is a giving soul — a forgiving, joyful, cooperative and optimistic soul.

Once I saw a child who made me understand what a child really is. He was five or six years old. He was about to eat his dinner which his mother had brought to him on a plate. He took the plate and sat down with it on the floor. As he started to eat, his little doggie came and began to gobble the boy's dinner off the plate. The child screamed in joy every time the dog swallowed the food. He was in great ecstasy, seeing how his dog was eating the food and wagging his tail right and left.

A few times the boy's mother wanted to put the dog out, but I whispered to her to just watch and share the joy of her child. As she watched more, a great smile and joy came over her face. After the dog finished the plate and he wanted to lick the child's face, as if to express his gratitude, the child's mother rushed over and lifted up the child with great joy and love, and began to dance with him.

Later she said to me, "I had never felt any joy like this toward him before. I didn't even know that he had such a joy in his heart."

He was a child, and if his mother had attacked him, she would have lost her joy and led the child into confused thoughts and feelings. The dog, which the boy loved, was eating the boy's food — and that was a moment of joy for him.

People are the victims of their own programming. This programming must change by developing a new psychology toward life. We must develop the psychology of joy. We must develop the ability to enjoy life and all that Mother Nature has for us. We grown-ups will never understand the psychology of the child, because we are complicated by our selfish interests and programming. Those who cannot be children lose the joy of life.

People, especially those who think they are educated, are living like old fellows under heavy burdens, self-made and self-perpetuated. Such "wise" people have led the world to the edge of Niagara Falls. Only a return to the child's psychology will help us avoid total disaster.

The greatest characteristic of a child is joy. Life is a joy for him; a little rock, a little branch, or a little gift makes him full of joy.

The second characteristic of a child is gratitude. Child psychologists missed this point. The most grateful person in the world is a child. He shows his gratitude in his joy. But remember that millions of children are psychologically starving, because of the greed and painful psychology of the world.

Once I was visiting an old-age home. People seventy-five, eighty, and eighty-five years old were sitting there like mummies waiting for the Stranger to take them away. There was a heavy sadness in this home. I talked to a few of them. They said they wanted to die as soon as possible. I stood in the middle of the hall and said to them, "I came here to teach you a children's dance. All of you stand up, hold each other's hands, and I will tell you what to do."

I taught them the steps of the dance and the music, and then we began to dance. We danced the dance five times. They were full of joyful tears. When I was leaving, they asked me to come again and dance with them. Later, one of the nurses said to me, "They had a great time, and finally they wanted to live and enjoy life."

Joy can be given freely, and as you give joy, you increase your own joy. "Unless you become like children, you will never enter the Kingdom of God...." People become grown-ups with their bodies and brains, and then build all that is necessary to destroy this planet. These people are not average people, but *grown-ups*.

Some people cannot remember events of joy before a certain age. This means that they have certain psychological barriers. Psychological barriers are those moments in which we had a negative shock, we were painfully rejected or ignored, or we were violently attacked at the time of the joy experience. At certain times, post-hypnotic suggestions act as barriers to our memories. But all of these things can be overcome if we increase the current of joy, which can wipe them out — slowly or with a sudden blow.

Rather than working on your painful memories, you can increase your joy flow in such a degree that your released joy, like rushing water, cleans all hindrances in your system. The memory can be restored, not only for one life, but also for many lives, if the obstacles are removed. In general, obstacles are violent deaths, massive disasters, treasons, murder, accumulated layers of pain and sorrow, despair and depression, violent physical attacks, sexual abuse, loss of money, property or beloved friends, and so on.

All these things can build barriers between the Treasury and the three permanent atoms, where all the records are hidden, and the brain. Increasing joy can systematically wipe out barriers and restore the communication system between the brain and the Treasury, or the memory disks.

Joy has a close relationship with memory. Increase joy, and you increase the memory.

I see many families sit in front of their television sets, watching movies of violence, murder, sex and immorality. Instead of wasting time and polluting their minds, they can sit down as a family and do the exercises of joy. Such a family will be healthy, harmonious, progressive, and even adventurous.

It is possible to release a great volume of energy into our systems, but sometimes if our systems are not integrated and aligned, that energy goes to the most sensitive centers and stimulates them. In olden days, when Great Ones used to contact Their disciples, They would advise them to fast first for five days, and work on some great projects so that when They contacted them, the energy would be used purposefully and goal-fittingly.

In a monastery after a certain meditation exercise, the teacher used to advise his students to sit and write a paper about some lofty subject. The reason for this was to direct the energy of love to the higher centers and not allow it to stimulate the lower centers. The teacher also advised the students to run half a mile and swim in the cold river every day.

It is important to notice, however, that such dangers do not exist for the *joy energy*. Let us remember that pure joy is "a special wisdom." You can increase this energy as much as you can and still be safe and protected, because joy energy carries with it its own wisdom and it energizes the whole system in a way that no harm is done to it. On the contrary, because of joy energy, many obstacles are removed from the system.

Being a harmless energy and controlled by wisdom, joy releases itself in such a quantity that we can cooperate with it and use it creatively in certain plans and projects. This is why when we are full of joy, we must think what we can do with this energy. Play or compose music? Write a book or a poem? Visit a friend in the hospital? Help a friend? Build a wall or a piece of furniture? Clean the house or dance?

It is possible to waste the released energy, or not use it at all, but enjoy it. If it is used or shared creatively, you not only increase the flow of joy, but you also increase your creativity and transform your being.

It is possible to use joy energy to contact Higher Worlds. We are told that when we are full of joy, angelic beings see great colorful rays in our auras and are attracted to us. Greater contacts with Higher Worlds are fulfilled during times of intense joy, if we are ready to use joy for building a path of contact.

Remember that joy is one of the highest substances found in our nature. If our consciousness is organized enough, it is possible to use this energy to build the bridge for continuity of consciousness, to charge certain centers, and to create around them a proper sphere to nourish them. This energy can also be used to repair certain damages done to our physical, emotional and mental vehicles.

Joy is a beam of life which can be used for any healing work in our systems. In the future, some advanced souls will be born and use the beam of joy for distant healing. They will be able to heal distorted and disturbed minds, emotions and diseases. They will be able to tune up the human system according to the laws and principles of life.

It will be possible by projecting the beam of joy to disperse hatred, animosity, fear, anger, jealousy, revenge ... to disperse crowds swayed by such dark tidal waves, and inspire heroic actions, cooperation, sacrificial deeds, and profound artistic and constructive labor. In the future, the science of joy will be the most advanced course in esoteric and scientific universities.

It is possible that a certain amount of accumulated joy energy can leak away. How does this happen? If you are with people who are surrounded by gossip, malice, slander, and treason, they can empty the container of your joy. It is also possible to lose your joy energy if you associate yourself with or live among those people whose lives are inspired by separatism, vanity, ego, pretension, hypocrisy, unrighteousness, revenge, greed, hatred, fear, anger, jealousy, worry, doubt, confusion, anxiety, panic, agitation, irritation, and so on.

You can also lose your joy energy by coming in contact with people who are contaminated physically, emotionally and mentally, or who are carriers of sexually-transmissible diseases. Such elements can disturb the flow of your joy energy — *if the flow of your joy energy is not stable yet and powerful enough to resist them.*

A joyless person resembles a soulless person. Joy increases if you try to dedicate yourself to sacrificial service, if you strive toward beauty and synthesis, and work for peace and cooperation. Every night before you sleep, fill yourself with joy and send joy to all who are striving on the path of perfection.

People can bring joy with them from past lives. If one is striving toward beauty, goodness, righteousness and freedom, trying to make his life a path of service for others, for many lives he will be born from those parents and in those places where his past deeds will evoke and release an ever-flowing amount of joy from his

Core.

To be more correct, sacrifice, service and striving toward beauty, righteousness, goodness and freedom will evoke the stream of joy which, life after life, will bring all those proper conditions in which the person's joy will grow, bloom, and flourish, spreading creative currents and glory all around him.

Reincarnation is a fact. People say that God is righteous, and here in the world we see miserable criminals and great humanitarians; we see stupid, insane people and geniuses. How can a righteous God create such extremes and throw the criminals into hell? This is totally illogical. How can God condemn something which He created?

Through such a simple logic, we say that it is man who makes himself great or miserable, with his thoughts, words and actions. Whatever he sows, he reaps. This is an unusual law. Joyful people are those who in the past tried to evoke joy, share joy, and distribute joy. A great artist is the result of many ages of striving toward beauty. Nothing is given to us without our efforts to obtain it. If in this life we talk, listen, read and think about joy and try to be joyful, in coming lives our joy will give its fruits. This is why the Ageless Wisdom says that it is never too late to start something new.

The benefits of joy never stop, if its flow is constant. The greatest mystery of joy is that you do not need to advise people on how to handle their lives constructively. Just teach them how to be joyful and how to share their joy, and joy will teach them what to do, how to do it, and why to do it. The mystery is that "joy is a special wisdom." When you have continuous joy, you can have all that is in harmony with joy.

We must also remember that joy increases your light, and light reveals to you exactly what you are. First, you feel horrified of yourself, because you start seeing horrible things in yourself that you never saw before. Then joy reveals to you the ways to overcome them. Then joy shines on your path more and more, like "the pillar of light."

Joy not only gives you wisdom, but it also makes you very

fast and sharp in your thinking. Read a book after you have taken revenge on someone or after you have hated or gossiped. You will see how confused your understanding becomes. But when you read a book in joy, you will not only understand the meaning of the words, but you will also penetrate into the core and the purpose of the book.

What is joy actually? To answer this question, we must go to the *Upanishads*, in which it is written that the Self is joy. God is infinite bliss. When a ray of bliss finds a mechanism in which it can still manifest its beauty, glory and wisdom, we say that bliss has manifested as joy. In other words, when the ray of bliss comes in contact with a highly-organized mechanism, it expresses itself as joy. It is this ray of joy that reveals the will and direction of the Creator. This means that those who have joy, those who live in joy and share their joy with others, those who try to make people joyful, have *direction* and *the Divine Will operates in them in the light of wisdom.*

As joy increases, the purpose of life appears more and more clearly, and man walks in light as the friend of the Source of bliss. Blessed are those who walk in the light of the wisdom of joy!

In the admission ceremony for a certain sacred Brotherhood, the Leader says to the neophyte, who is invited to be a co-worker in the Army of Light, "You who came to us blind-folded and without shield, you can now receive first the shield of joy, and then the spear of light." Co-workers must be shielded by joy. A highly-qualified group of people in any field of human endeavor who are dedicated to serving humanity, must be shielded, individually and in group formation, by the shield of joy. Unless they have the shield of joy, they will not be able to be used by the creative forces of the Universe, because they will be vulnerable to the forces of destruction.

The greatest battles against slavery, darkness, ignorance, corruption and totalitarianism are carried on with the shield of joy and the spear of light. Heroism and sacrificial service are inspired by joy, and the work is carried on under the shield of joy. A great sage, M.M., suggests that a psychological foundation must be established to make scientific research about joy.

Joy can exist in painful conditions. Joy is not subject to any condition. It may appear in the most happy conditions, or in pain, suffering, and sacrificial labor. The body and personality may be involved in painful conditions, but the heart lives in joy.

Joy helps you to detach your consciousness and withdraw into your inner castle, while the war is raging in the valley of your life. Joy also shields you and releases you on the battlefield to strengthen the hands of those who stand for beauty, goodness, righteousness and freedom.

Sometimes, besides the flow of joy from your Inner Core, additional joy is given to you from the Higher Worlds. In the Higher Worlds, joy is more substantial and real. Some of your co-workers from there project joy to you in your labor, when conditions become darker and more dangerous.

There is the joy of Infinity and endlessness. People lose their joy by involving themselves with transient objects and with values that live very short lives. But the concepts of Infinity and endlessness fascinate the heart with joy.

We create imaginary stations on the path of the endless journey, and we say that if we reach those stations we are perfect; if not, we are lost. But the path is endless. Perfection and achievement are not ends in themselves, but beginnings of something higher.

You can even think, speak or do something infinitely better, and better, and better. On the path there are stop signs, but they are obeyed only to give others a chance to proceed on their own infinite paths as they cross yours. Such a joy of Infinity and endlessness must be cultivated in you. You can experience it in visiting mountains and oceans, but you can make better contact with joy by observing the night skies with the millions of stars, or by thinking about Infinity and endlessness.

Our sense of values is distorted because our values are the products of the finite; they are the products of all those objects which are transient and exist only in time. When our sense of values is not balanced with infinite and timeless values, we lose our path and work for our own destruction.

From childhood, we must develop the balance between earthly and heavenly values. The joy of Infinity and timelessness is the joy coming from the infinite and timeless section of the human being. As this joy increases, the person is more and more charged with infinite and timeless values.

Another source of true joy is the conviction that the Elder Brothers of humanity exist as a collective beacon on our journey through the ocean of life. This joy can cause fantastic changes in our lives. In our darkest hours we feel the Guiding Hand. In any moment of discouragement, failure or attack, Their images cheer us up. We realize that we can also do a mighty service to humanity, as They did, passing through unimaginable assaults and difficulties on Their path.

It is such a great joy to have an Elder Brother or Sister by you, while you are walking through the deserts, mountains and jungles of life.

Joy expands our consciousness. Our expansion of consciousness has greater meaning for the world than for us. Each expanding consciousness becomes a leader of goodness, light and beauty. By each expansion of consciousness, the world is enriched. Through each expansion of consciousness, the Higher Worlds can make better contacts with the people living in the three lower worlds. The Universal Spirit rejoices every time we expand our consciousness.

The healing power of joy lies in its power to eradicate imperil and prevent irritation.[1] Irritation is the prime source of all destructive diseases. Imperil hides itself within many forms of illness, but increasing joy is the only power which can fight against them. Joy and wormwood oil together can perform marvelous healings, but when joy becomes fiery, no earthly measures are needed to fight against diseases.

Every day we must exercise joy, until all avenues of joy are

---

[1] For further information, read *Irritation—The Destructive Fire*, by T. Saraydarian

open within us. An Initiate of high degree is an embodiment of joy. A universal hero is not a man or a woman, but a stream of joy.

It is time that science investigates the influence of joy. We have in mind a pure joy, the joy of the good, the joy of creativity. Otherwise, all who live with ill-will feel happy imagining that their radiations are filled with light.

M.M.

Joy stimulates the glandular system. It is especially effective on the endocrine system. Major disorders of the body can be corrected by joy.

In the future, hospitals will have a special department whose members will prepare joyful events to evoke joy from the patients. This department will work in the light of science, and all events will be prepared in scientific detail to meet the needs of particular patients. Mental or psychiatric hospitals will be equipped with such a team of people.

It is very interesting to know that agents which are destructive to our mental health cannot survive in the radiation of joy. Many experiments will be carried on in people to see how certain chemicals differently affect people who are joyful, and people who are sad, negative, sorrowful, grieved, and so on. Machines will even be created which will be able to measure joy, accumulate joy, and transmit joy.

Once a person understands that joy is energy, he will not have difficulty understanding the above concepts. The mental, emotional and physical states of beingness under the influence of joy will be examined; then the secretions; then the heart; then the senses. Thought currents under the influence of joy will be measured. Actually, one can send better telepathic messages if he is in joy. The energy of joy combined with the energy of thought can perform miracles.

Love combined with joy is very much different than joy by itself. Sex without love creates a deep disappointment. One can have intercourse with love and enjoy the act, but if joy and love combine, the couple reaches ecstasy. Ecstasy is not a feeling or state of consciousness, but a moment of opening the aura into the Intuitional Plane, from which comes a beam of bliss. Ecstasy in sex cannot be reached by those who commit adultery, who change partners frequently, who are not faithful to each other, or whose hearts are divided. Long years of sacrificial and joyful relationship can open the gates of ecstasy. This is why sex is sacred. It can transform a person, if he is ready for it.

One must also observe that using any part of the body or senses without joy weakens that part and even creates complications in it. If you are having intercourse without joy, you will eventually develop complications in your sexual organs. If your eyes and ears are under the influence of the rays of sorrow and pain, even they will eventually lose their capacity to serve. If you cause pain and suffering to others with your hands, you will gradually develop many complications in your hands.

Once a man whose right hand was paralyzed came to our monastery. The Teacher asked him what he used to do most with his right hand. After pausing for a few moments, he said, "I used my right hand to slaughter sheep and bulls for many years."

"How many did you slaughter?" asked the Teacher.

"Thousands...."

I did not hear the rest of the conversation because suddenly the dinner bell rang. Later I asked the Teacher how slaughtering animals could paralyze someone's arm. He said, "Every time that man felt the pain and suffering of the animals, the life-giving energy decreased in his arm, and it eventually disappeared completely. Lack of joy causes paralysis."

In such a sophisticated age, people may laugh at this statement and consider it a superstition. But my Teacher healed that man's paralysis in six months by daily for four hours making him exercise joy. Once I copied down one of his exercises:

"Visualize your right arm, and with it pull a drowning man from a river.... Write a joyful letter with it.... Give money and jewels to the poor with it.... Serve food for hundreds of people with it...."

This man used to sit like a statue and follow the exercises

given by my Teacher for four hours daily. At the end of six months, he used that arm to give water to a mountain deer which was visiting our garden.

Some psychiatrists must think and research to find out whether such a cure can be scientifically explained.

Once after Christ healed the blindness of a man, the man answered to a crowd of doubters, "I know one thing: I couldn't see before, but now I can see." After such a realization, all arguments and doubts seem like the noises of a mosquito.

Most spiritual healers are charged with the energy of joy, and they can instantaneously transmit that joy and eliminate the causes of problems. I believe that in the near future, a great institution will be organized for the research of joy. First, all that has been said in the world about joy, in all languages, will be compiled and categorized. Second, scientific experiments on joy will be conducted. Third, the energy of joy will be used with the energy of love. Fourth, the energy of joy will be used as the laser beam of the New Age.

People will learn to communicate with each other through joy. They will learn how to communicate with Higher Worlds through joy. People must eliminate all painful images throughout the world, including painful movies, painful literature, and painful history, if humanity is going to penetrate into a higher dimension. A new history must be written for humanity, in which all the joyful moments of history are collected.

A joyful moment is a moment of freedom, beauty, goodness, or righteousness. This history must be written not from the viewpoint of any nation and not for any nation, but from the viewpoint of humanity and for one humanity, as joy cannot live in separative interests.

Human development and transformation are initiated and regulated by the Higher Worlds through certain energy currents. These special currents reach only those people whose auras are charged with joy. Joy in the aura gives extreme magnetic sensitivity to these currents and the power of absorption. Future, higher evolution will belong to those who live in joy, who share joy, and who spread joy.

A consciousness charged with joy is completely different from a consciousness which is charged with gloom. Psychic energy is assimilated and distributed only through joy. It is the joy in our hearts that brings in currents of psychic energy.

To compare psychic energy with joy, we can say that psychic energy is the Sun and joy is a ray of the Sun. The two always go together. One cannot contact psychic energy except through joy. Joy accumulates many kinds of creative and constructive energies from Space. It also gives people the wisdom of how to use these energies.

It is possible that great heroes of the Teaching spend their psychic energy in excessive service and deprive their blood of psychic energy. This, we are told, creates complications in the blood, and can even cause cancer. But exhausted psychic energy can be restored through joy — increasing, fiery, overwhelming joy. This is why workers in the field of service of light are advised to always be joyful, in order to replace their exhausted psychic energy.

Attacks come to workers when after exhaustion of psychic energy they fall into depression, loneliness or grief because of various attacks from people. It is very important that those who are engaged in great service have a group of people around them who are charged with joy and enthusiasm and who can protect them from attacks after a heavy, exhausting service.

When a person is charged by psychic energy, he can use that energy constructively, or destructively, through mixing that energy with his positive or negative thoughts. A person's psychic energy accumulates on whatever objects he touches, and stays there sometimes for a very long time. It is possible that certain objects are destructively charged with such a psychic and thought energy. Those who touch such objects feel various reactions.

When thought is energized by psychic energy, it becomes a factor of goodness or evil. But when joy joins with psychic energy and thought, it creates a benevolent character in the thought. No thought which is charged by joy can be destructive, evil or separative, but it is always constructive, benevolent and unifying.

Joy cannot be misused by evil thinking. Joy makes it impossible for the mind to think in evil ways. Thus the combination of psychic energy, joy and thinking, brings miracles in the life of humanity.

Beauty plays a great role in increasing joy. It is possible to charge oneself with joy through enjoying beauty in any form. The feeling of gratitude also releases a great amount of joy. Striving toward perfection releases the most hidden resources of joy.

Once someone asked a great Teacher, "Teacher, we are told that after leaving our bodies, we face a great darkness in the Subtle World. How can we see our path, and what kind of light can be used there?"

The Teacher answered, "There will be many kinds of light, but the most shining light and guide will be joy. Every time you experience pure, fiery joy, you light a candle on the eternal path, and when you pass away, you see beautiful candles lit on your path which increase in light as the joy of your heart touches them.

"Darkness never exists for those who sow the seeds of joy in their transient lives and reap columns of light on their eternal path. Joy is the guide to the Higher Worlds."

Another great Teacher, speaking about joy, says that one can also develop joy by exercising admiration. Admiration can release many fountains of joy within you. Try to have time to admire Nature — flowers, leaves, trees, mountains, rivers, waterfalls, lakes, birds and their songs.... Try to cultivate admiration for beauty, in whatever form it takes. Try to cultivate admiration for the skill and wisdom of geniuses and for the creativity of great artists.

Pictures, sculptures, books, poems, jewelry, physical skills — anything that is beautiful — must evoke admiration from you. Have a time every day for ten to fifteen minutes to admire something beautiful, intelligent, ingenious, or lovely. Nature and the whole world are full of objects of admiration.

If you are secluded in your room, close your eyes and visualize or remember objects of admiration. Remember remarkable sayings, poems, or people whom you admire. In fifteen minutes, you will charge your nature with pure joy and use it for the rest of the day in all your actions, feelings and thoughts.

Admiration not only fills all your nature with joy energy, but it also brings you peace, calmness and health.

One of the qualities of children is admiration. While a mother passes by a beautiful flower, the child sits by it and enjoys the beauty of the flower. Observe how children admire many things. Their admiration is a main source of energy and joy for them. Even during their sadness and crying, if they see something beautiful, they forget about their problem and begin to admire the object.

It is possible to change many negative things in children just by creating the opportunity for them to admire. It will be possible in the future for psychiatrists to use a technique or drill of admiration to heal their patients. Admiration is a great way to release the joy energy and make it integrate and balance the whole mental mechanism, with its subtle counterparts.

Observe those who are advanced in age and healthy; they have an outstanding quality — admiration.

Great Teachers warn us against belittling criticism, gossip, slander, malice, hatred and revenge, because these worms destroy our protective net of energies. These negative qualities devour the substance of joy produced through admiration.

Admiration fills your aura with higher substance, but in a few minutes evil gossip can eat it away. Many fools deprive themselves of the energy of joy by hating others and slandering their friends.

Joy and admiration are given to all human beings. Any one of us, on his own level, has many opportunities to be joyful in daily life. No one can limit your opportunity to be joyful. No one can prevent you from admiring. Thus, Nature gives you an opportunity to heal yourself, to transform yourself, to progress, and to elevate your consciousness — every day, everywhere.

Joy is the flow of bliss; happiness is the physical experience of joy. Thus, joy can be experienced on various levels as happiness, as pure or higher joy, or as fiery joy.

Bliss can only be experienced in very rare moments, like a flash of light. But those who can go beyond their mental vehicle and enter the intuitional sphere can live continuously in bliss. Nirvana is the gate of bliss.

Rapture is a moment when your soul is caught in the currents of bliss. The path to Home is the path of happiness, joy and bliss. Try to create a happy world, a joyful life, and a blissful striving toward the Highest.

Joy energy is the safest energy to cause transmutation, transformation, and transfiguration. It is very interesting to know that when one is exposed prematurely to assimilating beauty, goodness and truth, he creates resistances in his personality vehicles. This resistance produces friction and inflammation in certain areas of the aura, which become the cause of various diseases.

Beyond the human boundaries exist greater joys which are experienced by those who are able to free themselves from human and earthly limitations. There is the joy of bodilessness. There is the joy of being in Other Worlds. There is the joy of meeting Great Ones. There is the joy of witnessing the symphony of energies controlling a globe, a solar system, a galaxy....

Then there is the joy of being ready to participate in a superhuman labor — to see, to hear, and to understand in higher dimensions, to create in the world of fire and energy. The whole Cosmos dances in a sphere of joy.... However, the advancing soul knows that pain, suffering and destructive processes are everywhere in Nature. They exist to lead the steps of the traveler toward bliss, toward the Higher Worlds.

Some people are so depressed and beaten by the events of their lives that they do not want to remember the joyful moments of their lives. They even feel that to be joyful is really stupid. You can help such people in the following ways:

   1. Tell them about your own joyful moments in your

life.
2. Tell them true stories of the joyful moments of other people.
3. Help them by pointing out things in their lives for which they must be grateful and feel joy.
4. Pass on to them certain good news about national and international affairs.

If you catch such a person's interest with one of these points and gain his involvement and interest, you will have a greater success in creating joy in him. Do not press more; wait a few days and then repeat your technique again, with a brighter approach. Sometimes if the above techniques fail, you can use the following one:

Exercise For Creating A New Identity

Sit down and make a list of thirty good qualities about yourself. These must be qualities which *you* think you have, not things that other people tell you about yourself. Then for one month, take one quality daily and think for five to ten minutes about how you can improve or increase this quality in yourself.

At the end of one month, you will see that you will have built a solid identity in yourself. This is the identity which no one will be able to take away from you with their changeable opinions and ideas about you.

This exercise must be done with continuous attention on the virtue of humility. All the while you are building your spiritual identity, you must remind yourself that you will not show off your treasures, demand recognition for your beauty, or expose your values.

In addition, you must have a time to think about those things which may prevent you from developing your best qualities and which may hinder your progress. For example, say you have on your list the good quality of faithfulness or solemnity. You must think what can hinder the further development and expansion of your faithfulness or solemnity, or what might attack these qualities. You must also consider how it is possible to use faithfulness or solemnity for your selfish interest or desire for superiority.

Joy And Healing
Part II

Joy stimulates your glandular system. When you are joyful, you are strong and you can do almost anything. You can jump from one mountaintop to another. You even feel that you can fly to the stars.

Joy stimulates your emotional centers. When the emotional centers are stimulated, joy cleans and purifies your whole emotional system. Joy throws out all negative emotions. When you are joyful, you do not hate. When you are joyful, you cannot be angry; you do not even have fear. When you are joyful, you are not jealous or revengeful. This means that joy eliminates many bad things from your emotional realms. In a sense, joy heals your body and your emotions. Without joy, you cannot do anything constructive.

Joy coordinates and synchronizes the gears of your mental nature. It coordinates and integrates your physical body with your etheric body — the electromagnetic part of your body. Joy stimulates your glands.

If you are in the process of making a great decision in your life, do not become gloomy, narrow-minded, hesitant, fearful, or excited. Just be joyful, and you will see how right your decision will be. Unfortunately, most of the decisions that we make are made under pressure, grief, depression, fear, anger, or hatred. This is why most of our decisions are wrong.

Only those decisions taken in the light of joy will be right decisions, because joy expands your consciousness, synchronizes the gears in it, and eliminates dark thoughtforms, prejudices, superstitions, and preconceived ideas. Joy clears the mirror of your mind so that your Soul reflects the decisions on the lake of your mental plane.

When your physical, emotional and mental bodies are synchronized, aligned and purified, you are on the road to health and happiness. Doctors are slowly finding out that before they heal the body, they must give the patient joy. If you go to a doctor, he may tell you that your condition is bad or that you are in grave danger, and you may feel that you are going to die. But if your doctor tells you that there is a little problem which can be cured and not to worry, you are already on the path of recovery. It is the inner joy that heals you or helps the healing process.

Joy is not an emotional state or a physical or mental condition. Joy is energy. Man is a drop of God. Man is a Spark from God, and God is bliss. If you multiply joy ten million times, you may have a slight idea what bliss is. Whoever becomes blissful or joyful understands what God is.

God is not a hateful, jealous, revengeful, separative, aggressive, or destructive energy. Human beings often think that God is these negative things, but He is bliss. This is why the human being in all of his endeavors tries first of all to be happy, then joyful; then he tries to merge into bliss.

Happiness is the lowest expression of bliss. When you are happy, you want to be joyful; then when you are joyful, you want to be blissful. As Christ said, "Be perfect as your Father in heaven is perfect." This is the formula which helps people understand that Christ was referring to a mystery — that man must slowly become happy, joyful and blissful, as he goes toward perfection.

This is life's path. There is nothing else that you should look for. You buy furniture to be happy. You marry and have children because you want to have joy. You learn, feel, and try to do things because you want to be blissful. All of life is a search for happiness, joy and bliss.

Happiness is physical-emotional. Joy is mental-spiritual. Bliss is divine. You, in your own Core, are bliss. This is why it is said that if you find yourself, you will be the most joyful person in the world. Try to find your Core and touch your Core, because your Core is God. Nothing exists within you except God. Christ said,

"You are the temple and in the temple the Almighty One dwells." You are the temple of God.

You are going to find in that temple the living God. When you find it, you will see that you and He are one. Saint John said, "We don't know what we are going to be, but when we see Him, we will be like Him." This is a great mystery. Your destiny is to go slowly toward your Self, releasing the energy of bliss.

If the energy of bliss is sensed in your physical and emotional nature, it is called happiness. If bliss is sensed mentally and spiritually, it is called joy. If it is sensed beyond the lower bodies, it is bliss or ecstasy. It is samadhi, a state in which nothing affects you.

There is a story regarding the stoning death of Stephen, the first Christian martyr. As the stones were hitting his face, head, back and spine, he was in ecstasy. His face began to shine, and he was praising the Lord. The people present were surprised. He left his body and emotions behind, and was united with the Divine Purpose, with divinity. Nothing could attack him any more because he was in ecstasy. This has happened to many, many great souls, leaders and heroes. When they united with their divine counterpart, they were in bliss, even while in fire or under the sword.

Bliss is very far away from us. First, we must be happy; then we can have a slight idea of what joy is.

I wanted to know what science, psychology and philosophy said about joy. After searching, I found very little written about joy. To my knowledge, there is not a single scientific research study about joy and what it does for the body, the emotions and the mind, as well as for plants, trees, animals, and the whole environment, which also includes groups, nations, and the whole of humanity. Joy is really the greatest healing power, because it is the power of God, the power of your Spirit. You can heal yourself through increasing your joy.

I can tell you very sincerely that my body was really the weakest body, for certain reasons I do not know. But I healed myself continuously through joy. I would sit down and become joyful; ten minutes later, my pains, anxieties and worries were gone, and I was energized. You do not know how many dark arrows hit me — gossip, slander, treason — to make me feel smaller and smaller. One day I said to myself, "Get out of this grave!" "How?" "Through the light of joy." And I did it!

You will notice that your joy is affected by what you do to others. If you want to be happy, you do not steal from people and kill them. Searching for happiness improves your relationships. If you want to be really joyful, then do not have hatred, fear, anger, jealousy and revenge. But people say, "No, I want to be joyful, and in the meantime I want to hate and destroy." Eventually they find out that this does not work.

Let us say, for example, that you are feeling joyful; then the telephone rings and you start lying. Ten minutes later, you discover that your joy is gone. Satan and God cannot live together. In searching for joy, happiness and bliss, you slowly behave and correct your life. You improve your life and make it a process of moving toward perfection.

As our sun moves into Aquarius, all humanity has started to search for happiness. A few people who are more advanced are looking for joy and bliss. Of course, there are people who feel happy when they do something nasty to others or hurt them, but even such people are searching for joy. Psychologically, such people are very unhappy people, even sick people. They get themselves into many kinds of trouble and problems, eventually to find that joy cannot be theirs by taking the joys of other people.

People instinctively see a danger in those who attack the joys of other people, depriving them of their freedom, possessions, and joys. Eventually they try to discipline those who cause grief and sadness to other people. The prisons and asylums are full of people who tried in some way to rob the joys of other people.

Every time we deprive other people of their joy, we record these experiences in our psyche. These experiences slowly accumulate and begin to create certain pressure in our being. Often depression and heavy grief are the result of the pressure of such accumulated expressions, which become explosive.

Joy And Healing — Part II

Joy is a very important factor to keep units and groups integrated. Very soon people will realize that success in any business or group work dedicated to the human welfare depends upon the joy energy circulating in the personnel of the business or the group.

Joy not only elevates the individual consciousness, but also the consciousness of the workers and members of the group. It creates right attitudes of workers and members toward each other. It establishes right relationships among people. It gives enthusiasm and keeps the vision of service clear in their hearts.

If members of a group or if business partners raise the level of their joy with daily exercises, a substantial improvement will be seen in the business or group work. Those elements who bring negativity, depression and apathy into any group activity stand as barriers on the path of the success of that group.

A business can be ruined if even one key person yields himself to negativity or depression and loses his joy for his service and labor, his enthusiasm and vision. Great leaders and executives are those who in the most critical times still keep the flame of joy and hope shining in their hearts.

Joy must be introduced into schools and classes. The greater and deeper is the students' joy, the greater will be their understanding and success. My father had a "habit." Whenever he entered his pharmacy he would ask, "How are my boys? Do they work in joy?" and when leaving the pharmacy, he used to say, "Joy be with you until I see you again."

Once he told me that the prescriptions filled under the mood of joy were more potent medicines than medicines prepared by a person in a negative mood. If any one of his workers was ever a little on the negative side, he used to call him and look in his eyes for a few minutes. Usually the person would feel uplifted.

Once a worker told me that when he started to work for my father, the hardest thing about working in the pharmacy was being joyful all day. "But now," he said, "the hardest thing for me is to be without joy."

Once two workers had a little problem. My father called them to the office and looked at them with a deep smile. Then he broke into laughter and said, "Well, go to work." These two people left the office in laughter.... They saw how silly their problem was and how comical was their attitude toward each other.

Joy must be introduced into all departments of labor. People cannot substitute alcohol, food, and parties for joy. Joy must be evoked from the heart. A joy evoked from the heart develops a sense of transcendence in us, which protects us from falling into the petty problems of life.

Experiences of ecstasy are very rare. We do know that they are possible and that certain people have experienced them.

The first ecstasy that you experience is sexual ecstasy. Then there is the ecstasy of being sacrificial, the ecstasy of prayer, the ecstasy of service, creative ecstasy, dancing ecstasy, singing ecstasy, and so on. Joy in the lowest plane is felt as happiness. In the next level, it is joy, and in the next level, it is bliss and ecstasy. Rapture is intensified joy.

Slowly, you must experience such joys and create practical ways and means to experience more joy, more ecstasy, and more happiness.

The moment you are happy, you must observe what the happiness is or what the joy is, and what they are doing. There is happiness related to the body, to the emotions, and to the mind. You must find out which happiness you are experiencing. Eventually you will find out how the light of joy improves your life.

Joy makes you successful in your social life. If you really observe your social life — family life, partnership life, business life — you will find that those who are successful and fulfilled in their lives are joyful people. If your wife or husband is not joyful, you want to get rid of her or him. A woman prefers a husband who is joyful, even if he has little money. Joy brings light, health and happiness to your children and into your home.

I had a friend in school who was always depressed and in pain and suffering. One day I asked him, "What's happening?"

He said, "The world is no good; this is no good; that is no good; God is no good...."

I said, "Stop it!"

He used to try to bring me down into depression.

I always tried to show him the bright side of life, some beautiful qualities he had.... I even used to bring him some beautiful flowers and leaves, showing him how gorgeous they were. I used to tell him about heroes who brought joy to people.

One day I found him in the forest lying on his back, listening to the songs of the birds, and watching the huge trees. "What are you doing here?" I asked.

"For the first time I discovered that there is an immense joy in Nature.... I want to be joyful!"

This boy gradually healed himself by communicating with the joy of the beauty of Nature ... music, dance, and reading poetry.

One of the great sources of joy is the expansion of consciousness, through which the level of your being is raised up and detached from various identifications of the physical, emotional and mental natures. By expanding your consciousness and gaining detachment from the lower elements, you raise your beingness to a higher realm, closer to the Source of joy.

On every step of elevation you absorb greater joy and radiate greater joy. Freedom is gained only when your consciousness is in the process of expansion and your beingness is in the process of elevation.

You must select your partners, friends, wives, husbands, boyfriends, and teachers from those who have joy, because joy is a sign that they are not average people. If they do not have joy, be very careful; they can poison your environment. Depressed people always create problems around themselves.

Depression leads you toward failure, separation and conflict, while joy leads you toward success. Be joyful with your friends. If you have problems, start doing something humorous or joyful; then start discussing your problem. You will see that even before you discuss it, the problem has disappeared. Problems cannot be solved in the darkness of depression or anger. They must be solved in the light of joy. That is why a great sage says, "Joy is a special wisdom."

Most human beings do not have joy in their homes, schools, shops, factories and offices. This is totally wrong. Without joy, we cannot have success or render service. To a great degree, people have tension, strain and fear in their relations with each other. That is why, as a nation, we are not advancing as we should.

If you visit any public office and observe the faces of the employees who work there, you will be horrified. Very often there is a great lack of happiness, respect and cooperation. A nation advances if joy is spread in the hearts of its people. Try to intelligently spread joy, because joy uplifts your nation, your family, and your group. Joy prevents groups, nations and individuals from going in the wrong direction. Joy always keeps you headed in the right direction, toward success.

The first major thing that joy does is to make you successful. Once while I was in the Royal Air Force, I was told to select a sergeant from ten candidates. One of the candidates came into my office and said very coldly, "What can I do for you, sir?"

I said, "Go away."

Another candidate came to me and said with joy, "Good morning! Isn't it a beautiful day?"

I said to him, "You are going to be the sergeant."

When I was a child, maybe three years old, we had thirty to thirty-five very tall, black shepherds working for us who came from Africa. We had five thousand buffalos, which they herded. Once a month the shepherds returned to our home from the herds, and on those occasions, they played with me in great joy. I was always waiting for them. When they came, they made a large circle and I became their "football." They would lift me into their hands and throw me up like a ball, from one man to the next, maybe fifteen times. It was a great joy to fly above their heads.

One day I had a very bad cold. My mother said, "You are not going to leave this room. You must stay in bed and drink all the medicine I give you." While my mother was in another room, my little sister came to me and said, "The blacks came."

"Wow!" I said, and immediately jumped out of bed and ran to where the shepherds were. When they saw me, the circle formed. I had a fever and I was very sick, but I was flying in the air. After ten rounds, they sat me down, and the fever was gone! My mother said to the shepherds, "What did you do? You killed the boy!" They said, "He is fine. There is nothing wrong." I did not have any more pain or fever. It had vanished in my extreme joy.

This happened a second time when I was thirty-six years old. I had a very bad cold and a high fever, and my wife said, "Stay in bed." Then the postman brought me a letter from Alice Bailey. In the letter it said, "We are taking you into a special group for advanced studies." After I read that letter, my fever, headache and pain totally disappeared. I got up, got dressed, and started to write and organize my papers.

My wife came in and said, "Are you crazy?"

I said, "No. Everything is fine. Look at this letter." The letter brought me ten tons of joy, and the joy healed me.

Look for joy in your life, and try to see what is happening to you when you are ill or have other problems. If you review the few days previous to your difficulties, you will find that you were depressed and unjoyful. Being unjoyful is how you catch sickness. If you are charged with the electricity of joy, you can even enter into nests of microbes and not be affected by them. But if for only one moment you feel depressed or full of self-pity, you will attract the microbes. Remember, joy makes you healthy and successful.

Joy makes you victorious. You conquer obstacles if you have joy. You must enter into battle with joy. A sage says, "My friends, take the sword in your hands in the name of joy." You must enter into the battle with joy. By the word "battle," we are not referring to war and destroying people; we are referring to the battle against your own hindrances, limitations and ignorance, as well as against the situations and conditions that are making you sick and depressed. Enter into every kind of spiritual and moral fight with real joy, and you will see how successful you will be.

Once there was a student who failed his exams three or four times. I asked him, "How do you take your examinations?"

He replied, "Well, naturally I am already trembling when I enter the room. Then I feel afraid and angry, and I hate everything."

"You have vipers all around you," I said. "How can you successfully take an exam?" I gave him one or two hours of exercises of imagining that he was entering the examination room with great joy and confidence. The next day he passed the exam he had to take. Later, he said, "I was really intelligent that day!"

Let us say that you are scheduled for surgery. Go with joy to the operating room, and you will see what a difference it makes. If you are going to have some teeth pulled, do not panic. Laugh and say, "These are my diseased teeth. Let them be removed. I am so joyful!" Create ten or fifteen exercises before the surgery, seeing how joyful you are when the teeth are coming out. You will be amazed how fast you recover. The doctor will tell you that the wound should heal in one week, but you will cure it in one day! These are the miracles that can be performed through joy.

If you have a daughter or son who has problems, do not use anger, fear, hatred, jealousy or revenge with them. Just use joy. Speak with joy, play with joy, and you will see how they improve.

Whenever your mouth is foul-smelling, it is an indication that you went through a depression and you were not joyful. Start being joyful and your glands will clean everything. The body will be normal when you have joy. Joy does this because to be joyful means to really be in your natural environment. You are, in your essence, joy. Do not forget this.

If you compare five people's faces, those who do not have many wrinkles and who look bright and shining are those who have had the most joy in their lives. Wrinkles are found on the faces of those who have passed through tribulations, suffering and pain, without the secret of joy.

In the future, the Olympics are going to use these concepts. Before athletes are accepted into the Olympics, they will go through a process of charging their physical, emotional and mental systems with joy. When they have joy, they will excel in the various events.

Once one of my friends, a very gifted violinist, had suddenly fallen in love with a girl. "Falling in love is dangerous, especially for violinists," I said. He replied, "No, I love this girl."

One day after that he was giving an important recital. He asked, "Is my girlfriend here?"

"Yes," I said, "she is sitting in the back. But she doesn't want you to see her." (I was lying.)

"Good," he said.

During the first half of the recital his playing was masterful. Just before the second half, he said, "Where is she? She did not come backstage at intermission to see me."

"She is not here; forget it," I said.

All during the second half, his playing was lifeless and flat. When the program was finished, he went backstage and took his violin and destroyed it. In one moment when his joy disappeared, he destroyed his violin. He never touched the violin again. That girl destroyed him, or rather, he destroyed himself, just because the girl had a problem and did not come to his recital that day.

Joy is so important for your life, but very few people talk about its importance. If you are joyful, everything you want to know, you will know, because God works through joy. "I give My joy to you," Christ said. What a secret sentence this is, if you really understand what He meant.

How Do We Increase Our Joy?

When you do a service for someone without expectation, you increase your joy. Giving, not taking, increases your joy. Taking increases your happiness, but it does not increase your joy. Give something, and you will see how your joy increases.

The most miserable people are those who are greedy. Greed is when you have and have and have, until you are suffering with the pain of fearfulness, hatefulness and separativeness. Start giving, and you will increase your joy.

One day an eighty-two-year-old man gave two hundred million dollars to scientific research. After he had given the money, he said, "I feel joyful for the first time in my life." This was good, but do not wait until you are eighty-two years old to start giving. Start helping others today. Give and serve to people, and you will increase your joy.

One day I was asked to visit a couple at their home. The man said, "This woman is detestable." The wife said, "He is like a mule. We cannot live together."

I went to the kitchen to get a glass of water. I did not want her irritation to come to me, so I helped myself. The kitchen was so dirty and chaotic. I said to the woman, "Don't you clean your kitchen?" "No, let my husband bring a servant," she said.

"Oh," I thought, "that is the source of the unhappiness." They were each waiting to be served by the other. I went into the other room and told the man, "If you want to save yourself, start cleaning the house and show her how much you can give."

It worked. One month later the woman said, "I guess that I must clean the house, not my husband." "Ahh," I said, "things are going better and better now." They are still together.

Serve your husband; serve your wife, and you will bring

How Do We Increase Our Joy? 61

happiness to your home. Daughters and mothers must serve each other. For example, the mother says to her daughter, "The kitchen must be cleaned." "No, Mommy, I am watching television," says the daughter. That mother is going to be a little "sour" inside. Her negativity may increase and turn into hatred, separatism and rejection. In such ways, the poisoning of the home begins.

We can see that joy is the most effective energy that changes our lives, individually, in the family, and in the group. Joy puts things in the right condition, and in these right conditions, you feel happy, joyful, and sometimes blissful.

For example, if you conduct research in asylums or prisons, you will see that those inmates who suffer from the most severe physical, emotional and mental diseases and failures are those who came from homes of sorrow, conflict and pain. Some children can respond and change the situation, but most of them fall on their faces. When parents are very joyful, they charge the "batteries" — the whole system — of their children. In this way, the children become successful adults.

It is time now to increase joy, which is the opposite of depression, pain and ugliness, so that you balance and overcome the negativity, and begin a new life in joy.

Bliss, joy and happiness exist within you. You do not have to search outside for them. For example, you may say, "I want to be happy, so I will desire an expensive car, a palace or a million dollars." Day and night you desire the things which you think will make you happy; you go through stress and strain, and then have a heart attack and die. This is not the happiness that we are referring to.

Happiness is an inner condition, an inner state of consciousness, an inner feeling. Let us say that you do not have much money, but when you look at the beauty of flowers and appreciate the beauty of Nature, you feel happy and joyful. Happiness, joy and bliss are within you. The only thing that you need to do is to bring them out and manifest them. Searching for joy, happiness and bliss outside of yourself leads you totally in the wrong direction. Release your True Self, and you will be flooded with joy, bliss and happiness.

The first way that you can increase your happiness, joy and bliss is to do sacrificial service for others. The greatest sacrificial people, such as Christ, Buddha, Krishna, Confucius, and Lao Tsu, always suffered, but They were at the same time joyful. What was Their secret? Through sacrificial service, They released the Inner Core, and flooded Their systems with the energies of that Inner Core — the Inner Self, the Inner Divinity, the inner source of creativity.

An artist feels very happy when he creates, because he releases the creative joy that is within himself. Joy must be looked for inside oneself.

Striving toward beauty is the second way to increase your happiness, joy and bliss. Striving toward beauty is a state of consciousness, a state of awareness, and a state of appreciation and enjoyment of beauty that starts releasing the joy within you.

Any time you are a little depressed or down, think something beautiful and you will see what will happen. The joy will increase and overcome the unhappiness that you have. When any difficulty comes, do not face it with anger, hatred, and revenge; first become joyful.

Friends of the great Mogul ruler, King Akbar, said to him one day, "King Akbar, we found two very sneaky 'rattlesnake' enemies for you." He replied, "I am so happy! Now I have an opportunity to demonstrate my greatest creative powers to overcome these enemies." By declaring this, he had already overcome the obstacles.

The first step in striving toward victory is joyful acceptance that there are problems to be solved. Then because you have the confidence to solve them, you will be joyful that there are problems and that you have the opportunity to prove your ability to solve them.

Striving toward synthesis is the third way to increase your happiness, joy and bliss. Striving toward synthesis means to take many, many things that are not related and build a whole concept or a unit out of them. For example, three opinions are totally different. Can you relate them in a way that they make sense together and offer the solution for the problem? If you do this, you will see how much joy will come and flow out from your Inner Core.

Christ said something very mysterious: "Blessed are the peacemakers." Peace is the secret of bringing two opposing and contradictory things into harmony. When you are peaceful, there are no conflicting parts in you. A nation is peaceful when there are no cleavages in it. Make peace within yourself. When you make peace within, you will feel joy and you will synthesize yourself.

To synthesize means to compose a symphony with many hundreds of notes. You bring the notes together in such a way that the sound is symphonic, synthesized. Synthesis leads you into joy. Separatism and cleavages lead you into unhappiness.

If you are fighting with your boyfriend, girlfriend, partner, or anyone else, you are unhappy. But if you create synthesis, peace and understanding, you are happy. Through increasing the joy of others, you increase your own joy.

Make others happy, and you will be happy. Do not make yourself happy at the expense of others' happiness. Do not base your happiness on your money, positions or possessions, but let the foundation of your happiness and joy be your Inner Core. Give more joy to others, and you will be more joyful.

Light is the result of contact between joy and matter. When joy has contact with your body, it creates happiness. When it comes into contact with your mental body, it creates light. This is why every time you have more light, you have more joy.

For example, let us say that you solved a difficult mathematical problem. Were you more joyful? Of course. This happened because light was created when the joy was in contact with your thoughtforms or thoughts, and the mental body.

You are going to awaken the giant sleeping within you. This giant is joy and it cannot be released as long as you are begging for joy from outside sources. Always remember that joy increases when you give it to others. You can give joy by expanding the consciousness of people, or rendering a good service for them, or elevating their spirits through wisdom and the Teaching.

Once Christ was approached by His disciples, who said, "Master, when You pass away, don't forget us because we want to become generals and statesmen in Your kingdom."

Christ said, "In My kingdom, I will remember you."

Because He is King, He will remember the disciples. Then He said, "The kingdom of God is within you." He meant that the "King" is within you. If you want to be a king, search for Him.

Joy is within you. This is what you must realize.

Seven Qualities Of Joy

*T*he energy of joy has seven qualities:

1. **Joy is a regenerative energy.** It regenerates your whole physical, emotional and mental system. When you feel a little weak, start thinking about joy and you will see what will happen.

2. **Joy is a purifying energy.** It purifies your mind, your emotions, and your body. Have you noticed that people often gossip when they are depressed, negative, or unhealthy, or when they have complications in their lives? I have never seen a joyful person who gossips. When people are joyful, they do not want to hear gossip. They often say to the gossiper, "It is not a problem; I love him." An elevated state of consciousness does not like to hear gossip.

3. **Joy disperses your cloudy mental, emotional and physical atmosphere.** It disperses your worries, anxieties, grief, greed, and so on, just as the sun disperses the clouds and you have a sunny day. The Inner Sun, the Inner Divinity within you Whose nature is bliss, disperses the clouds.

4. **The Teaching of the Ageless Wisdom brings joy to people, because it pulls out their souls from the common life, in which they are attached to transient objects of pleasure.** On the other hand, some people see a mysterious phenomenon. They see that as they go deeper into the Ageless Wisdom, their lives enter a turbulence in which, instead of depression, their joy increases. The reason for this is that the Teaching pulls out all hidden suppressions and releases them onto the surface of your life.

Sometimes a time comes when you see how miserable you are, and how helpless you are in confronting your life. But you also feel the presence of joy in your life. Such a condition may last for one

life or for many lives, or luckily for only a few years. If the latter is the case, it would be most beneficial to:
  a. abstain from sex;
  b. engage in heavy physical labor, running, swimming, or climbing;
  c. not meditate or study;
  d. speak as little as possible;
  e. think a lot about joy.

Joy is sometimes called the life-book of conquerors. Observe how the outer structure of your old life is wiped away, and see that it is because of the removal of the old structure that your inner beauty emerges triumphant and in great joy.

5. Joy expands your energy field. It expands your positive emotions. When you are joyful, you jump and hug others. When you do not have joy, you sit there like a sack of potatoes.

Joy expands your mind and creative abilities. When you are joyful, you create the best dance, the best painting, the best music. If you are grieved, your creative mechanism is paralyzed. If you are going to give a lecture, do not let anyone give you bad news just before you speak. When you receive bad news, your balloon becomes like a flat tire. Ask someone to tell you something very beautiful. Then when you start to lecture, you will see how your lecture will improve.

I tested this. Once I was preparing for a seminar when a man told me about a very tragic event. I arrived at the lecture hall very depressed and shocked. Finally, I told my friends and staff, "Don't ever give me bad news before I lecture or perform musically. I do not want anybody giving me negative news at these times, because it brings me down."

If you have friends who really understand you, you can be a creative artist, a talent, a genius. You must have three or four people around you who keep you in good humor before you perform; then you will see how you will bloom.

Once there was a young girl who was a very talented violinist. Whenever she would start to practice, her mother would say, "Oh my gosh, again the violin!" The whole family used to tell her when she started to practice, "Keep it short." Eventually they killed her talent. She needed three or four hopeful, joyful people near her encouraging her, instead of wishing they did not have to listen to her.

Joy expands your consciousness. Expansion of consciousness is very important because you are equal to your consciousness. Joy expands your consciousness and understanding.

Joy encourages. Gloom discourages. Gloom develops jealousy and discouragement. If you are dancing, gloom says, "So what? It is not so good. Other people can do better than you." This is the psychology of the opposite of joy, and it can be seen everywhere.

6. The energy of joy makes things unfold. You can cause unfoldment, development and expansion in people through joy.

7. Joy is a burning energy. It burns impurities in your physical, emotional and mental system. The sage D.K. says, "Humanity until now has lived a life of suffering and pain. But God is sending new messengers who, instead of preaching and talking about suffering, pain and crucifixion, will talk about joy, happiness, bliss and resurrection." The New-Age teaching must be based on joy and resurrection, not on crucifixion. Christ was crucified for only two or three hours, but He has been resurrected for thousands of years now. Why are people still talking about crucifixion instead of resurrection?

The Spirit is resurrection. The body can be crucified, but not the Spirit. It is better to start looking at these things in a new light. Beauty is the formulation of joy and bliss.

Old-age teachings stress guilt. Guilt is identification with your mistakes and failures. If you have joy, you will never identify with failures.

Once a young boy broke a large jar. Because he was so joyful, he started dancing around the jar, saying, "So what?" He was not identified with the mistake that he made, because he was joyful. If that boy had not been joyful, he would have sat and cried, saying, "Mommy is going to beat me...."

Why are you not seeing God in every human being? You are so beautiful, even with all your mistakes, because God within you is going to conquer those mistakes. You are developing; so what if you made mistakes in the past?

Hindrances
To Joy

1. **Separatism creates hindrances to joy.** If you are separative, you are against God. Whenever you are separative, joy disappears from you. When you are really joyful, start gossiping and you will see how unhappy your heart will be. When you are joyful, steal something and you will be unhappy. When you are joyful, do something unrighteous and you will see the joy evaporating from your heart.

If you unify and synthesize people, your joy will increase. If you divide people, your joy disappears.

2. **Vanity works against joy, because vanity is a labor to build a false self-image within yourself.** Vanity is the assumption that you have lots of things which you do not have, that you know lots of things which you do not know, that you can do many things which you cannot do.

Vanity works against joy. For example, if you have preconceived ideas and superstitions, or if you are brainwashed, you will not want to change yourself and orient yourself to reality. In such a case, joy will not abide within you. But if you see yourself as you are and if you can expand your consciousness to see reality and try to improve yourself, your joy will increase.

3. **The ego is against joy.** The ego says, "I am important; you are not. Everyone must worship me. I am the most important person." The ego is very touchy. If anyone "touches" your ego, it aches. Leave the ego alone, because it blocks the flow of bliss energy.

4. **Pretension is a hindrance to the flow of joy and bliss.** Pretension means to pretend that you are something which you are not. When you do this, you feel contradictory waves within yourself, fighting against each other. Your conscience says, "You

are not," while your mind fabricates, "You are." This creates cleavages within you, and you cannot have joy when you are divided within yourself.

5. **Hypocrisy is the worst enemy of joy.** Hypocrites are the most unhappy people. Of course, everyone has some degree of hypocrisy in him, but we must try to overcome it.

In the Teaching, hypocrisy is condemned as a great obstacle that leaves man deprived of having contact with the Higher Worlds. Hypocrisy is a form of acting, imitating and pretending. Such efforts build a barrier between the person and the world of joy. This barrier grows to such a dimension that it deflects every ray of contact from the Higher Worlds, or every ray coming from the world of essence and joy.

A hypocrite distorts reality through his personality, and he cannot come in contact with reality through his essence. His essence remains poor, and his personality runs the show. Eventually his personality becomes him (the essence), and his essence dries up. Thus we say that a hypocrite commits suicide in betraying his essence, the source of his joy.

You can see "actors" on every level of human society. It is these people who occupy their positions to prevent qualified people from transmitting reality to society. The busiest place for "actors" is in religion. Religion could not cause real transformation in this world because of hypocrites of many colors.

It is easy to act as if one represents a Great One, but it is immensely hard to keep away from hypocrisy and be a true transmitter of the Teaching of a Great One, through a life lived according to the essence of the Teaching. Joy flows through a person who is simple, straight and real.

6. **Revenge, greed, hatred, fear, anger and jealousy are all enemies of joy.**

7. **There are also five physical enemies which sap our joy: contamination, pollution, wrong action, harmful action, and destructive action.** If you have any of these things, you cannot have joy. Keep yourself away from these enemies.

70 Hindrances To Joy

Joy increases through faith. Increase your faith, trust, inclusiveness, sincerity, simplicity, clear thinking, and righteousness. Meditate, observe and discipline yourself. This is how you can cultivate the garden of joy.

Peace and tranquility increase your joy; be peaceful. Harmlessness increases your joy. Every time you do a harmful act, physically, mentally or emotionally, your joy evaporates. Aspiration increases your joy. Aspiration is a drive to have a higher state of feeling, enjoyment and experience. Devotion increases your joy. In devotion, you focus all your heart into a great beauty.

Health increases your joy. If you are not healthy, you lose your joy. Dynamism and enthusiasm increase your joy. If, for example, you are washing your dishes with hatred and anger and cursing them, your joy evaporates. But if you are laboring with enthusiasm, you increase your joy. Labor, right action, right sleep, right sex, and right diet, all increase your joy.

How To Use Joy

1. **The first way to use joy is through your thoughts.** Do not allow any thought that is not joyful to form or build itself in your mind. Do not allow in any thought that is not optimistic or that does not expand your hope and future. Any time you build an unjoyful, negative thought in your mind, you have a "worm" or a leakage there. For example, if you are going to create a new business, a work of art, or anything creative, do not think, "What if I am not successful? What if I fail? What if things go wrong?"

Joy can be spread through your thoughts. Joyful thoughts carry tremendous amounts of the charge of joy, which can transform your business, your future, and your plans, as well as the plans of others. Maybe eighty percent of your thoughts are not joyful. They are gloomy, sad, painful, and centered around failures, struggles, hatred, revenge, and so on. Do not cherish these negative thoughts. To learn how to prevent negative thoughts, you must simply start preventing them. Start learning how to make your thoughts be joyful thoughts.

Try to observe yourself today, tomorrow, next year, and for the rest of your life. See if you can change your negative thoughts into positive, joyful ones. For example, let us say that you know a person who did something or said something that upset you. You start the motor of negative thoughts, which produces poisonous exhaust fumes. Try to stop this process immediately and say, "Can I think good about her or about him?" You think that negative thoughts are going to hurt him and that in this way you can take revenge. But before the thoughts leave your mind, they have already polluted your own aura. Your negative thoughts hurt you before they hurt the other person.

This is why some churches use affirmations. Affirmations are mechanical, but they help change the course of the thoughts. If you have negative thoughts, they distort the mental mechanism because they are poisonous. Mental energy is neither negative nor positive; it is indifferent energy.

When the thinking process starts, it is your motive that causes that energy to build forms which are either poisonous or regenerative. Before you think, say, "This thought is going to be a very healthy, beautiful thought." Ugly thinking is one of the causes of your defeat. Negative thoughts, poisonous thoughts, and unjoyful thoughts prepare your defeat.

Positive, right or beautiful thoughts are joyful thoughts. Joy is a spiritual energy. If your thoughts are charged with joy, they will be invincible, victorious and powerful thoughts. They will nourish your mental body, your physical body, and your aura. These are the secrets of Nature, but people do not talk about them.

You worry, "By what sickness will I die? Am I going to have an accident? What will happen to me? Do I have cancer now?" All of these thoughts are circulating in your mind. Kill them with joyful thoughts. Try to start thinking opposite thoughts: "You know, I am going to live a very long, happy, healthy life. I will be so beautiful. I am pure, intelligent...." When you do this, the electrical system of your body starts to work in positive gears instead of negative gears.

You are either killing or shaping yourself. You are the one who is killing yourself; you are the one who is healing yourself. If you have negativity in you or if you are pessimistic, you are poisoning the atmosphere in which you are living.

2. Have joyful plans. Never plan anything that is painful or causes harm to others. Create harmless, joyful plans. For example, say, "I am going to plan something good. When my husband comes home, I am going to have a nice dinner prepared, with flowers on the table. I am going to use positive speech." If you are a husband, you must plan how to make your wife and children happy.

When you start planning things that are constructive, harmless and beautiful, you nourish your mental mechanism with joy energy. This is how you become more intelligent. Poisonous plans are harmful to your intelligence. Even if a person is your enemy, plan something beautiful when you meet. Always create joy and joy-producing plans. Your mind must enter into a new "gear" in order to understand these ideas.

Try to face reality with joy. Try to discover yourself and all about yourself with joy. Any event or situation that reveals your nature to you must be a moment of joy.

When you face yourself with joy, you will not identify yourself with your mistakes and errors; you will not build an ugly image of yourself in your consciousness. Instead, you will raise yourself to the level of the observer — with non-identification.

If you have a leadership or teaching position, you do not need to use anger and fear to correct people's behavior. You can use joy, letting people know that it is a great advantage to know about their own faults, so that they use themselves in a better way for survival, success and service. Every time you force your ugliness, your pain and your suffering on others, you prepare terrorists around you.

If you want to teach people the Higher Teaching, first make them love you. After they love you, you will not have difficulty teaching them; they will accept you. For example, do not plan to damage or destroy people. On the contrary, do good things for them. Once I counseled a woman about her relationship with her husband. She hated him and he hated her. They had been living like this for five years. The woman said, "You know, I now have two lawyers. I am going to fix that man."

I said, "How much money are you going to spend?"

"Oh," she said, "at least five thousand dollars."

"You can do it spending only a few dollars," I said.

"Okay," she said, "tell me how you can do it and I will listen to you."

"What does your husband love?" I asked her.

"He loves shish kebab, wine, clothes...."

"Good," I said, "his birthday is coming up. Take these things and make a feast for him, and you will see what will happen."

She did, and the man changed. Now they worship each other. Show love and joy; then you will "win" without the courts. But you must always be sincere.

Send gifts. In this way you break all opposition. But we do not often do this. Usually we start with negative attacks and add more negative attacks. Then we spend money, money, money to fight others. With these methods there are no positive results. This is why a Wise One says not to fight against enemies with the same ways and means they use. If you hate me, I cannot create a right relationship with you by returning hatred. Instead I must love you so that I change your hatred into love. But it must be intelligent love, good love, balanced love. If we hate each other, we waste money, time and energy. Remember, joy solves problems.

It is not easy to understand the full intensity of this topic all at once, but here and there you can see that your mind will start using joy in times of problems. If you use joy to solve your problems, they will be solved. For example, when one of my five children used to need money, she would always come and ask for it from me joyfully, and I would always give it to her. I would even give her more than she asked.

Your actions must be joyful. People do not like to be around those who curse as they work, with negative mannerisms and expressions. They want to be with people who bring joy to their work and their homes.

Once while in a restaurant, I was seated across from a young man and his girlfriend, who were very tense. The waiter brought their food, but he gave the wrong plates to the wrong people. The woman shoved the dish toward the man and said, "Here! Yours." And he did the same to her. They continued their meal looking as if they were going to attack each other. It was poisonous to look at them.

Try to do actions joyfully, not only for others but also for yourself. I know many people who curse as they iron their family's clothes. I visited a lady's home one day and found her ironing ten or fifteen shirts. She was singing and in the meantime, reading a book. She said that she often read inspiring books while ironing.

Dress joyfully. When you dress, put on your clothes with joy, not with irritation. If you observe your face and others' faces when they talk and move, you will see so much sadness, negativity, tension, and stress. Try to release yourself from these things! In this way, you create an atmosphere in which you can breathe.

Try to use joy in your families, with your friends, with your boss and with your co-workers. Try to work with the magic of joy. Joy is the key to success.

Once on a flight to Europe, I encountered a group of flight attendants who were very negative. Whenever we asked for anything, they would say, "Humph, here." Everyone on the plane was feeling the tension. The next time I traveled, I flew on a different airline. After twelve hours in the air, the attendants were not even tired; they were joyful and dynamic. When departing, I said to the captain, "This airline is the best because there is joy in it!" He was so proud.

Someone should write airline executives and managers to tell them that the best way to improve their business is to teach their personnel to spread joy.

M.M. says, "When We receive a letter, We psychologize it." There exists a special electrical machine that, when placed on the handwritten lines, projects them onto a screen. It shows how much energy the writer put into his letter. Some letters are dead, and measure below zero. Other letters are fantastically charged with psychic energy.

Whenever you write a letter, try to put psychic energy into it. Psychic energy is love energy and joy energy mixed together. Write your letters in joy and in love, and you will see what will happen.

One day I was very depressed, when a letter arrived from an eleven-year-old girl. She wrote, "You think that nobody loves you, but Christ loves you and I love you." Suddenly everything changed. I took the letter so seriously because it was handwritten, and she really meant it. Put joy in everything you do — in writing, thinking, feeling, touching, hugging, and in a firm handshake. Sometimes I shake hands with people whose hands feel almost dead, because there is no energy there.

Another thing which is very important is to daily send joy to your body. Early in the morning, say, "This body is going to work all day in very tiring and challenging conditions — in smog, noise, poison, freeways, red lights, and so on. Let me charge this body." Then close your eyes and fill your body with joy energy, and you will do better throughout the whole day.

Next, fill your emotions with joy. Say, "Today all my emotions are going to be joyful. I am not going to accept any failing, negative or painful emotions. All my emotions must be joyful." Of course, times will come when your emotions will challenge you. When this happens say, "Hey, you stop! Since early in the day I promised to have really good emotions and good thoughts, and I am going to keep my promise." Early in the morning, charge your physical, emotional and mental bodies with joy energy.

One of the secrets of joy is that every success is based on magnetism. Magnetism brings you the right man, the right woman, the right co-workers, the right boss, the right lawyer, the right doctor, the right dentist. Magnetism is the result of joy. No one can be magnetic unless he or she has joy. Therefore, the first thing to do early in the day is to charge your body, emotions and thinking with joy. All day you are going to radiate joy and create magnetism. This magnetism will make you successful in life.

If you have a problem with someone, do not meet him with irritation, anger or hatred. First, fill your being with joy and optimism. Then say a few good words regarding your approach. Then approach the problem with joy, respect and simplicity. You will be amazed what a difference it will make. Can you imagine

Christ going to the crucifixion with sorrow? He was so joyful that everything was going as planned.

Charge every object that you are using with joy. Hold your pencil and put the electricity of joy in it. In the future, scientists will find that the joy vibration still exists in such objects. Sediments of joy and sorrow always exist on the objects that you use. For example, someone gives you a pencil and for the next five days you are very uncomfortable. Then you find out that the pencil was used negatively and destructively, and it is now creating many kinds of disturbances in your electrical system. You must throw that pencil away.

I remember once a lady said to me, "For one month now we haven't had peace at home. Someone gave me a green object, a piece of jade, and then our trouble started."

"Who gave it to you?" I asked.

"A medium," she replied.

"Ahh," I said. "Throw that jade away, and your house will be all right."

Remember that your magnetism and electricity are accumulated in everything you touch. This is how cats and dogs can find you. Eventually special machines will be able to locate you by your frequency, not your fingerprints. The machines will register your frequency by examining an object which you have touched.

It is important to charge everything with joy. There is a very beautiful ceremony in the Armenian church, which I have not seen in any other church. Before the service, the priest enters a special room where he puts on the vestments. First he takes a white shirt and says, "May the joy of the Lord be in this shirt so that I wear it as a victory for the Forces of Light...." Then he puts on the next article and says another prayer and blessing. As he puts on each remaining vestment, he charges it with joy, blessings and bliss. Finally, he puts on the slippers and says, "With these slippers I am going to serve the Lord on the altar." Everything he wears is now blessed.

You feel so differently when you are dressed in such vestments. It is as if you are really somebody else, all because of the blessing.

Bless and charge with joy everything that you touch — the chairs you sit in, the clothes you wear, the foods you eat, the pencils you use, the books you read, the beds in which you sleep, your husband, wife, boyfriends and girlfriends. Bless everything around you.

Many religions, including the Christian, Jewish, Buddhist, and Zoroastrian religions, have the tradition of blessing the house in which you live. The priest comes and blesses the house before the family moves in. Blessing, in this sense, means to bring joy energy into the home. Such a house is different from other houses because it is blessed. It is blessed not by cursing, but by bringing joy into it.

Money is sometimes the most cursed thing. Money is an accumulator of psychic trash. For example, a single one-dollar bill has passed through thousands of unknown hands. Besides microbes, viruses and germs, money has poisonous psychic accumulations on it. Before you use money or put it in your pocket, bless it. In this way, the money is purified.

We are talking about energy. By that energy you can charge certain things. People say, "He has a green thumb." If you know people who have a "green thumb," you will find that they are joyful and the seeds that they plant contain the psychic energy of love and joy. This is why such seeds and plants grow best.

Once when I was a boy, my aunt and I planted some tomatoes. Those tomatoes grew so well because we were very joyful when we planted them. But if you plant in cursing, in hating, in fear, in revenge, or in a bad mood, those seeds are already killed by your negative, anti-life currents. Be joyful with your books, letters, gifts, and everything that you are using and sending.

When you start putting the ingredients together for cooking, bless them. Give a joy-charge to them, and you will see how nutritious the food will be. The only nutrition that exists in the world is joy. Everything that is nutritious has joy in it. When you take joy out of food, it becomes dead material. In the future, scientists will prove these things.

The best way to bless something is to put your two palms on the object and feel joy; then suddenly feel that joy is flowing out from your palms. It might take three or four minutes before you can feel it. Close your eyes and experiment. Whenever you feel that joy energy is flowing out from your fingers, bless the object.

Suppose that some parts of your body are ailing. Most people dislike everything that is painful, so their first reaction is to say, "You stomach ... you this ... you that!" This is the wrong attitude. The correct method is to send joy energy to your organs. Do not send joy directly to your physical organs; send it to the etheric counterpart of the organs. The etheric body contains the counterparts of all your physical organs. Every change that occurs in the physical body occurs first in the etheric body. From the etheric body, the change transfers itself into the physical body, except in the case of accidents.

Let us take, for example, the stomach. If your stomach is bothering you, imagine an etheric stomach one foot away from your physical stomach. Then work on the real stomach, the etheric stomach, seeing it totally healthy and happy in the energy of joy. In this way you can regulate, repair and heal yourself. Then two or three minutes later, the real, etheric organ will condition your physical organ.

When you send your joy energy directly to the physical body, it may create a reaction, because you generate too much energy for the physical body to absorb. In this way, you bypass the etheric body and thus do not heal yourself. Your work should be with the etheric body, not the physical body. The physical body is an automaton — like a shadow that changes as the object which creates it changes. Your etheric body is the reality, and its shadow is your physical body. Your etheric body is real, and the physical body is the shadow.

Every sickness and every disturbance starts first in your etheric body, then spreads to your physical body. However, if you have an accident, someone shoots you or you fall down and cut yourself, and so on, the damage does not start from the etheric body; it starts from the physical body.

Sometimes after surgery when the incision has healed, you still feel pain. This is because the etheric body has not yet healed, and it is trying to adjust itself to the different physical conditions. Sometimes these pains last for three to seven years, until the new etheric atoms replace the old atoms.

Let us say that I had surgery on one of my fingers. The surgery is finished and the finger is healed, but still there is pain. This is because the etheric counterpart of the painful finger still exists. When the dense physical body is healed, I must do mental healing to heal the etheric body. I must say to the etheric body, "The physical finger is healed; now you must heal." And with joy, I will heal it. Immediately when you heal the etheric body, the physical body feels no pain.

Actually, it is not the physical body that registers sensations, but the etheric body. For example, a paralyzed arm has no feeling in it because its etheric body has withdrawn.

Anesthetics detach the etheric body from the physical nervous system. Between the physical body and the etheric body is a layer of fumes; this is the anesthetic. When the anesthetic wears off, the etheric body again blends with the dense physical body. The etheric body, not the dense physical body, is the life principle or the sensitive principle.

People speak about etheric surgery. In principle, it is possible, but there are few people who can do it. On the other hand, there are many charlatans in this field, as there are in other fields. Once I observed a man doing real etheric surgery. As he was performing surgery on the etheric stomach, he was seeing the counterpart of it, the dense physical stomach, cleaning and purifying itself. The patient is now eighty-four years old, and he feels like he is twenty-five.

More Exercises
On Joy

*A*ny time in your life that you are happy, joyful or in ecstasy, certain parts of your system register and accumulate that joy energy. Because of this, you have many "pockets" of joy in your system. We call them circuits of joy. They are in your aura. These circuits are encapsulated, however, by negative events, thoughts and feelings. They are no longer usable. Because they are not usable, they become encapsulated, crystallized forces in your aura. They actually become disturbing agents in your aura. This encapsulated energy can be released and made to circulate in your aura with a very simple method.

Let us say, for example, that when you were six years old, your daddy brought you a ball and it made you very happy. This happiness is a circuit of joy in your aura. But later, Daddy beat you or scolded you. At this point, the joy became encapsulated; it is not usable anymore. You must try to release this accumulated joy in your system so that you regenerate your system, your consciousness, your mind, and your emotions.

EXERCISE A

1. Relax and take three deep breaths. Imagine a moment of joy — a joyful experience that you had this year. Make it one complete experience. First remember the experience; know it. If you can remember it clearly, try to re-experience it as if you were going through that experience for the first time, feeling all the joy, ecstasy, freedom and beauty that you originally had.

If you finish it, repeat the experience again until you release every particle of it. Now find another moment or experience of great joy and try to re-experience it or re-live it.

Do this first with the experience of a physical joy, for at least twenty minutes.

2. Repeat the exercise, re-experiencing an emotional joy.

3. Re-experience a mental joy for twenty minutes — an experience of creativity, reading, thinking, speaking, and so on.

EXERCISE B

1. Visualize a mountain on which you are walking. See the mountain filled with flowers, bushes, greenery, rivers and waterfalls. Try to experience a tremendous joy in your system, as if there is nothing that bothers you. Feel the flowers; smell them. Touch the bushes. Listen to the birds; lie on your back and listen to them. Let everything go and just feel joyful.

2. See the light between the leaves of the trees. See a little bird coming close to you, and touch him. Now see that your body is lying on its back, and you are watching your body. Jump to the top of a tall tree and see a whole valley there; everything is very beautiful. Look at your body just lying there like a piece of wood.

3. While on the top of that tree, start to sing something beautiful that you love. Sing loudly so that every creature can hear it, especially foxes!

4. Now imagine an event that will give you the highest ecstasy and joy, and dramatize it. Maybe it is meeting someone, or receiving a check for fifty million dollars, or seeing your immortality.... It must be something that will make you very joyful. Create an event now. If you can create an event, it means that you can use the joy energy. Just imagine what will make you the most happy person.

5. Go to the top of the tree again. Imagine to whom you can send a ray of joy. Send it to your friends, mother, father, people who are alive or dead. Send them joy, like a beam of light. See how you are changing their natures. Do not judge them; do not rationalize anything; just send joy. Do not think about the results either. Just send joy — to sick people, depressed people, unsuccessful people. Be a fountain of joy.

6. You are on top of the tree again. Look down at your body and send joy to it, to every part of your body, etheric and physical. This is very important. Do it seriously. The color of your joy is violet. Pour a violet light on your body. See that light purifying, energizing, uplifting, integrating and totally healing it.

7. Again start with your head. Send a tremendous amount of energy around your head. Now send energy to your shoulders, your chest, from the top of the tree — do not forget that — looking down to your body. Send energy to your stomach, to other lower areas, to your legs, to your toes. Now see your whole body resting in a sphere of violet light.

8. Come close to your body and turn it on its stomach. Holding your hand five inches above the spine, go over the spine, charging the spine with violet energy. Starting from the bottom, come to the top of the head. Go slowly, like you are massaging the body in the air above it.

9. If you see that there is any dark cloud around the body, send a blue light and destroy any grey accumulation. Then see that the light around the body is all violet again.

10. Stand at the side of the head of your body, and take seven deep breaths. As you take seven breaths, see yourself as a lighted entity growing in light and energy. Then see a diamond in your head; that is the seed of the joy. See the diamond shining more and more and flooding all of yourself — your body — with light and joy.

See the diamond again, and see how, from the diamond, a pure violet light is coming and transfiguring all your vehicles.

11. Make your body stand up, and you stand at the back of your body. Raising your hands, channel blue energy to your body.

12. Stand in front of your body. Channel orange energy into it. Now stand on the right side, and channel yellow energy into it. From the left side, channel green energy, and see your body really healthy and dynamic. Burn every kind of germ that can exist in the body.

13. Rub your hands together. Touch your face and open your eyes.

Do not do these things by yourself, until you know what you are doing. There is nothing in the world more powerful than your Self, if only you can understand and learn the techniques to use that power which is within you.

You can do these exercises better if you have a friend near you to remind you of your every step and help you do the exercises thoroughly. But your friend must not criticize or advise you what to do. He must only read the instructions and give you ample time to follow each step. This friend can be called the "reminder."

It is also possible for you to record the instructions for the exercises, and follow the tape throughout the exercises, whenever you have one or more hours to do them. Each exercise can take five to twenty minutes, according to the time you have. If you do not have time to do all of an exercise at once, do a part of it the first day and another part the next day.

We are sick and tired of being "average animals." It is time now to be human beings. Our goal is to leave the "animal" behind, and then to leave the human being behind, and come next time as superhuman beings.

Exercise C

1. Close your eyes again. Imagine a success, an enterprise, a special work, or something that you are planning to do. Visualize your future. Visualize that you are becoming whatever your vision is for yourself. Visualize what you want to be, and visualize yourself becoming that somebody. Visualize that your highest dream is actualized.

2. Repeat Exercise C several times, for thirty to sixty minutes.

Exercise D

1. Feel extreme joy throughout your body, emotions, and mind. Build joy itself. Sense what joy is. Feel joy in your toes.

Feel it in your legs. Feel it in your hands. Feel it in your bones. Feel it in your arms, abdomen, chest, spine, neck, face, tongue, and your head, inside and out. Now feel joy all over yourself, the complete unit. See joy radiating out.

2. Radiate out joy as much as you can with all the parts of your body. Just radiate like you are a radioactive material. Raise your hands and send joy to the whole globe. Imagine every trouble spot in the world and send joy to it. Start with America, then go to Europe, the Middle East, the Far East, Asia, India, Russia, China, Japan ... and bless even the fishes in the ocean.

Sometimes you may cry in joy. There are joy tears and sadness tears. The chemistry of these two types of tears is totally different. The chemistry of sorrow tears is poisonous; they taste salty, while the tears of joy taste good, even delicious.

Your glands either circulate various poisons or bliss energy. Sometimes sweat can heal people. Once someone wrote about a girl in Armenia who puts her sweat on people's backs and makes their pain disappear. People have discovered that there are vitamins and other elements in sweat. This is the sweat of joy. But the sweat of guilt is poison.

Try to be joyful. Make your life a journey of joy.

Meditation On Joy

*I*t is very important to cultivate joy in the field of our consciousness, by sowing seeds of joy in it. The seeds of joy will bring a great harvest, not only individually, but also collectively. The meditation on joy will run as follows:

Every week have a short period of time, say fifteen to twenty-five minutes, and dedicate it to cultivating joy.

1. Relax physically, emotionally, and mentally.
2. Inhale joy deep into your being, and exhale joy. Do this three times. Then relax again for a moment.
3. Focus your consciousness above your head, and visualize a beautiful rainbow between two mountains.
4. Let the beauty of the rainbow fill your whole nature with additional joy.
5. Meditate seven times (once each week for seven weeks) on the following seed thought:

    "Joy is harmony between the Self and the Cosmic Self, emotionally sensed, intellectually approved, intuitionally actualized."

6. After meditating for fifteen to twenty-five minutes, record your thoughts and experiences in a special notebook.

On the night of the same day, have a review on joy:

1. Relax. Close your eyes, and ask the following questions:
    a. Was I joyful all day?
    b. What effects do I see in my nature and in the natures of those with whom I relate?

    c. Did I see the wisdom of joy in action?

    d. Do I see any relationship between joy and the clarity of my consciousness?

2. After you finish the review (twenty-five to thirty-five minutes), record your findings in your notebook.

You can also use your notebook to record any experience about joy which you have during the week.

It is good to change your seed thought of joy every seven weeks. The following seed thoughts are presented to you for your own use. You can meditate on them periodically, over and over again.

1. "Joy is a special wisdom."
2. Joy is bliss in manifestation.
3. Joy is energy, and it obeys certain laws, as electricity does.
4. Joy wipes out negativity and conflict within my nature.
5. Joy creates right human relations.
6. Wherever joy is, there can also be seen the presence of beauty, goodness, righteousness and freedom.
7. Joyful thoughts travel farther and more deeply into the Cosmos, and they evoke constructive and creative energies.
8. Joy affects plants, trees, objects, and human beings, and helps them to unfold and develop harmoniously.
9. Joy accumulates those energies which are used to travel to higher spheres.
10. Joy evokes peace.
11. In the fire of joy, no evil can exist.
12. Joy exists and increases in sharing it with all living beings.
13. Harmlessness is the forerunner of joy.
14. Perfection is achieved in ascending the ladder of joy.

"Joy Is A Special Wisdom"[1]

Joy is the fragrance of the Chalice, the Lotus. As the petals of the Lotus unfold, joy radiates out of the petals and gives vigor to the physical body, magnetism to the subtle body, and serenity to the mental body.

The Lotus is the permanent source of joy. As It unfolds, joy increases. Joy is not conditioned by outer circumstances; it is like a beacon, the foundation of which rests on ageless rocks.

Happiness is an effect of outer conditions. When favorable conditions change, happiness disappears, leaving the gloom of depression. Joy never changes. It increases as the problems and conflicts increase in one's life. It grows in spite of conditions.

As the experience of the pilgrim increases, as the field of his service expands, as he wills to sacrifice more and more, as he conquers more territory in self-realization, the fragrance of the Lotus increases and spreads over vaster areas.

The most attractive energy of a server is his joy, which radiates from his manners, from his voice, and through his eyes. Whatever he touches, blooms and unfolds.

Joy is not a feeling, nor is it an emotion; it is a state of consciousness, a state which is detached from the domination of the three lower worlds. The problems of these three worlds cannot reach it. Knowledge, love and the dynamic energy of the sacrificial petals spread out and charge all the tiny lives of the lower vehicles with the energy of joy.

Joy is not the absence of hindrances, problems and difficulties. On the contrary, joy is the flash springing out of each victory

---

[1] Agni Yoga Society, *Fiery World*, Vol. II, para. 258.

earned by the inner man through these obstacles. Joy grows in battle, in conflict, in service, in sacrifice. Real joy creates crises and tensions, and overcomes them. This is how it grows. It is joy that overcomes all hostilities and doubts, and builds numberless bridges between hearts.

Joy gives courage, inspiration and vision. It purifies, heals and sanctifies.

In the light of a joyful person, people see themselves as they are. All shadows of doubt disappear. They become inspired by a greater vision. The energy of courage starts to flow through their nerves. They make difficult decisions, and joy inflames their hearts toward greater beauties. Joy uplifts them and makes them more able, more free and more radioactive. No one can hurt you if joy is there. Black arrows from visible or invisible worlds fall down in front of the fortress of joy. Joy is harmony; that is why black arrows cannot penetrate it.

Any attack against joy produces depression, gloom, darkness and failure. Any communication with joy uplifts, exalts and beautifies.

Joy is the alchemical stone. It is the path to life, to love, to light. It is the magnetism of the Sun. Locked doors and fenced paths open to the presence of joy.

You can understand the expressions of joy in any language. From any level, you can translate them into your language.

A joyful person is the simplest person, the most straightforward person and the most profound person. You always understand him, but you always find something deeper in him. When you unveil one depth, another depth opens. Through the simplicity of joy, you are led into the mysteries of joy.

Success is the result of a labor which is carried on in joy. Start your work with joy, and the path of success will open in front of you. Communicate with joy; work with joy. Be joyful in all of your relationships, and even observe your failures with joy, in joy. Any failure observed in joy changes itself into success and victory. Any problems observed in joy dissolve. Joy is for Infinity. Joy is for changelessness. Joy is the witness of the imperishability of the human flame.

The form of the warrior's salutation for the New Age will be: "Rejoice!" This is not a handshake or a hello. This is not a kiss or an embrace. It is an act of charging people with the energy of joy. It is an act of uplifting them from the waves of the three worlds and holding them in beauty, in gratitude, in courage, in hope, in vision, and in reality.

"Rejoice!" Joy is the fragrance rising out from the Inner Chalice, an ever-singing melody.

In great humility, in great simplicity, enter into the Inner Sanctuary and see the Chalice. Look at the flame in the Chalice, the fire of bliss. Place your lips on the Chalice and taste the contents. Then enter into the ecstasy of love, of joy, of bliss.[2]

---

[2] Excerpt from *The Science of Becoming Oneself*, Chapter XXVIII, by H. (Torkom) Saraydarian.

How To Bring Love And Joy To People

Disciples have an inner fountain of joy and love which streams forth into their lives and nourishes people around them. Very often it is the joy and love of a disciple that attract people to the path of enlightenment and labor.

People sometimes think that joy and love are sentiments, feelings or emotions. The Ageless Wisdom teaches that love and joy are particular kinds of energies which have three fundamental tasks in the human kingdom:

1. They make life-forms exist, create and survive.
2. They help the formation of the soul, or the identity in man.
3. They create the atmosphere in which creativity in its highest meaning becomes possible.

The Ageless Wisdom teaches that love and joy are two great Cosmic Lives which are related to each other. Together They nourish all lives in the Cosmic Space, to make living forms survive, to help bring into existence the conscious unit in the human form; to make the soul exist; and to make the seeds of beauty unfold, bloom and flourish.

Without love and joy, life will disappear from the Earth. It is love and joy that make plants, flowers and trees survive. It is love and joy that make animals continue to exist. It is love and joy that make the human race continue living. Take away the energies of love and joy, and our planet will turn into a moon.

It is love and joy that keep a family, nation, and humanity together. Without love and joy, people will become suicidal. Love brings people, nations and lives together, and builds the mechanisms of survival. Joy makes the mechanisms expand, be inclusive, bloom, and express all their potentials of creativity.

The two energies, love and joy, are feminine and masculine. They penetrate into each atom and cell and try to inspire them and conceive in them the possibility of growing and surpassing their limits. They have similar effects on each form, on each family, on each nation, and on humanity.

Those individuals and nations which have more joy and more love last longer and help others to progress and enjoy life. Wherever these energies are withdrawn, crime, suicide and destruction set in.

We are only aware about love and joy in the vegetable, animal and human kingdoms; but love and joy exist in higher kingdoms, too, in a purer state and with greater power. It is love and joy that hold the stars in a constellation together. It is Cosmic love and joy that orchestrate the dance of stars in a Cosmic symphony.

Once a great Master said, "A deep joy is felt in heaven when one of you turns toward light."

Through joy, people greet each other. Through joy, recognition is expressed. Through joy, gratitude is offered. Through joy, the soul travels toward the Source of his origin.

Joy turns into bliss in higher realms. It is in bliss that all suffering, pain and separation vanish, and man feels one with all that exits.

The transformation of people starts not through knowledge, but through joy. The deeper you enter into joy, the better is the human being who forms within your shell. The tragedy is that we do not know how to penetrate deeper levels of joy, and that because of our ignorance we prevent people from penetrating into the spheres of joy.

Joy regenerates your system, your body; it purifies your emotions; it transforms and enlightens your mind. It helps in the formation of the pearl which we call the human soul.

The first thing that the energies of love and joy do is to condition the continuity of life on this planet.

The second thing they do is to nourish the immortal human soul, when they fuse with each other in a human being. It is after such a fusion that man becomes an individual, a living soul, instead of being a machine. This stage is called the formation of the pearl in the human heart. Until that pearl is built, you have no conscious immortality, although you do exist, as everything else exists.

Those who are not souls are like little pebbles in the river of causes and effects. They mechanically serve as causes, then become effects. This continues for a very long time, until love and joy are assimilated and the unfoldment of the soul takes place.

The apparatuses through which the energies of love and joy function are:

1. the etheric, astral and mental vehicles, through which survival becomes possible;
2. the heart center, in which the formation of the soul takes place; and
3. the Spiritual Triad, in which the human soul unfolds his Divine Will.

After the soul is unfolded in the heart, love-joy energy operates in the Spiritual Triad and manifests as bliss. Bliss evokes the hidden Core in the human soul, and the energy of the will is conceived in the human soul. It is these three energies combined which make possible the manifestation of the beauty hidden in the human Core. The beauty of Christ, Buddha, Zoroaster, Hercules, and other giants of humanity is manifested in this secret chamber of the inner pyramid. Great artworks in all forms are manifestations of these three energies: love, joy and will.

Once such a combination comes into existence in the secret chamber of the human soul, the person turns into a living beauty who evokes beauty from anyone with whom he comes in contact. It is in the Spiritual Triad that conscious immortality is achieved.

Unless we climb step by step toward survival, toward creating the soul, toward beauty and immortality, life will make us attach to superficial objects and forget our divine heritage. Without love and joy, the world will fall apart.

How to Increase Our Love and Our Joy

The law is this: Love increases in loving more; joy increases in giving more joy to others. Laws always have two sides — the "promotive" side and the restrictive side. The restrictive side of the law says that when the substances of love and joy do not gradually penetrate into all departments of the human being, they do not nourish the three fundamental tasks of life, and instead create imbalance in the human system.

In simple words, if the substances of love and joy are absorbed only on the personality level, they help for survival, but they do not go to the heart and create the individuality — the pearl, the soul. If they do not go to the spiritual level to create beauty or the manifestation of will that is in the Self, the All-Self, the evolution of the human being stops.

In practical terms, to increase love and joy we must know how to live and how to arrange things to increase these energies. Every effort to harmonize energy needs an apparatus. These apparatuses must be built and be ready to function, in order to accumulate energy.

The first apparatus — the physical, astral and mental bodies — is built: when one overcomes habits and lives a clean life; when he conquers all negative, painful emotions; and when he eliminates from his thinking all harmful thoughts. The second apparatus — the heart center — is built, nourished and unfolded through love energy. The third apparatus — the Spiritual Triad — is built through a life of joy in sacrificial service.

Once I asked my Teacher, "Are there people who live longer than average people?"

"Yes," he said, "I have seen people who are one hundred and twenty-five, one hundred and fifty, one hundred and seventy years old. I have even heard about people who live four hundred years, and of some who never die."

"What do they eat?"

"Their main foods are love, joy and hard labor. The more love, the more joy, and the more labor you *are*, the more life you *are*. Think about that."

How To Bring Love And Joy To People 97

Everything that is against love, against joy, and against labor, shortens life. All harmful thoughts, emotions, words and actions that are accumulated year after year, make our life shorter, painful and joyless. Hatred, separatism, anger, jealousy, revenge, malice, slander, fanaticism, ego — all of these germinate because of the absence of joy, love and labor. Crime is the absence of joy, love and labor.

One of my Teachers used to call love, "oxygen," and joy, "hydrogen," and labor, "water," that help flowers and trees to bloom. Thus, joy is fire and love is fire, and when they are combined in the right proportion, they create water — the creative fire.

This fire must always progress from physical to spiritual levels and circulate between these two poles, if we do not want it to hurt us and be used destructively. If love and joy do not continuously circulate and rise to the highest levels, they damage us.

For example, a lady says to you, "I love you, and because I love you, you must do all that I want you to do."

You say, "Lady, wait a minute. Love does not impose itself." She does not understand you, and she hates you. What happened? She said she loved you, and now she hates you. The reason is that love energy was stuck in her body and her emotional world, and it could not rise.

Our greatest enemies were once upon a time our friends. They became our enemies because we tried to let the energy of love climb up, but love energy was stuck in them and was serving a separate interest. Thus, a disciple becomes a Judas; wine turns into vinegar....

How must we protect the personality to absorb love-joy and increase will substance in our vehicles, to make them survive in this life for a few hundred years and continue surviving on other levels? There are three rules we can follow:
1. Elimination of all kinds of expressions of hatred, jealousy, revenge, fear and greed.
2. Elimination of all kinds of expressions of separatism, vanity and ego.

3. Elimination of all kinds of cruelty and harmfulness.

With these three rules, we must engage ourselves in the labor to cultivate:
   a. forgiveness, deeper love and compassion. (Understanding love is compassion.);
   b. contentment and gratitude; and
   c. inclusiveness.

When these three psychic apparatuses are in operation, they will absorb the substances of love and joy from Space.

What are the practical steps?
1. Anything which you feel is against love and joy in the expressions of others or within yourself must be approached first with the analytical mind, asking yourself the following questions:
   a. What makes him (or me) think that way, speak that way, write that way, or be that way?

   After asking this question, try to search for as many answers as possible. If you are frank and sincere with yourself, this will lead you to the *causes*. Try to approach this question with no anger, hatred or fear, so that you do not distort the mechanism of your seeing eye. Ask:
   b. What does he (or do I) want to accomplish with such behavior?
   c. Whom is he (or am I) trying to serve?
   d. Can I give a little dosage of love and joy and make him "wait a minute" in his downfall?
   e. How can I formulate and express my love and joy so that I do not create resistance, vanity, superiority or congestion in him?

   In trying to answer these questions, you pull yourself out from the emotional sphere and prevent an emotional reaction. Thus you do not disturb your inner apparatus.

2. The second step is to sit in meditation daily. Relax, and focus your mind on a pink-colored sphere of energy with violet waves, and inhale it into your whole being. Visualize love-joy being absorbed into your body. As you exhale, visualize it purifying all your being from thoughts and feelings that are harmful, ugly or shameful.
3. The third step is to make a list of:
   a. those to whom you can send thoughts of love and joy;
   b. those to whom you can send thoughts of love and joy through letters; and
   c. those to whom you can send thoughts of love and joy through certain gifts — money or objects.

When these three steps are carried on for a period of one year, you will see three things happening to you:

- You will feel more health and have more strength.
- You will create a focus in yourself, an integrity which is the formation of the soul.
- You will feel the breezes of an inner bliss, which will uplift you above all agitations of life.

People have an erroneous opinion that joy and love increase if one lives in an atmosphere of joy and love. These energies increase in our system not because they exist around us, but because of the quantity of joy and love we put out into the atmosphere. We become easily saturated with joy and love if they are poured out abundantly upon us. Such energies can even paralyze us and make us invalids, if we do not express the corresponding amount of love and joy.

We can increase our joy and love in places where they are not in existence. People complain and say, "We are living in a place where there are malice, slander, hatred, negative and destructive feelings, and all of these emotions are having a destructive effect upon us." This is very true if we do not react with love and joy, and take the conditions as a proper state in which to develop love and joy.

The law is this: You increase your love and joy by giving them to others who do not have them, in a way that you evoke from them love and joy and make them experience the value of love and joy. You make others aware of how love and joy increase if they are given out to those who do not have them.

To love does not mean:
- a. to surrender to weakness;
- b. to accept things that are harmful;
- c. to tolerate laziness;
- d. to encourage weakness and irresponsibility;
- e. to accept ugliness;
- f. to exploit people; or
- g. to put people into sleep.

To love means:
- a. to call forth the sense of responsibility;
- b. to point out weaknesses people have;
- c. to challenge people to strive and attain;
- d. to make people work on their habits and other weaknesses to eliminate them;
- e. to make them learn how to cooperate and overcome their egos;
- f. to make them engage in great labor for humanity; and
- g. to teach them how to overcome their vanities.

You cannot lead people into such labors except by the energies of love and joy. In putting your love and joy into such a labor, you increase them.

True love and joy increase in adverse conditions.

To give joy does not mean:
- a. to flatter people;
- b. to bribe people;
- c. to please people;
- d. to yield to people's appetites and habits;
- e. to allow people to deceive you; or
- f. to allow people to follow a destructive path.

How can we give greater joy to others?
  a. by making them see facts;
  b. by giving them vision, hope and future;
  c. by teaching them how to solve their problems;
  d. by helping them to contact their Inner Watch;
  e. by helping them to increase their creativity;
  f. by making them be grateful, giving and sharing; and
  g. by helping them to give joy to others.

When you love, you have joy. When you have joy and love, you become creative; you have purpose, because you have soul. When love and joy increase in you, you feel the urge to act, to work, to labor, and to manifest the beauty and glory of the Inner Self.

Various conditions are necessary to release the fountain of joy within you:

1. When your consciousness is in the process of expansion, you feel great joy. Every new level of consciousness puts you in contact with new and higher realms, where you realize the changelessness of your Core.

One of the enemies of our joy is fear. Fear disappears when a person finds in himself the Changeless One. The Changeless One is found only through expansion of consciousness. The closer you come to your Core, the greater is your joy.

The Changeless One is the Immortal One, the Permanent One. The awareness of permanency is a great source of joy. It is the impermanency of things that makes our joy disappear. Impermanent life, impermanent body and health, impermanent conditions, possessions, money, friends, wife and husband.... It is this impermanency that is the cause of all our fear. Once the Permanent One is found through expansion of consciousness, joy replaces fear.

Man must have a changeless reality in order to keep his sanity. For some people it is a Cosmic principle, a God, a Soul; for others it is immortality, the Self, the Core. When a person identifies himself with something impermanent, he becomes impermanent. Then when changes start in the impermanency, he loses the fulcrum and becomes insane.

This is why great Teachers always try to inspire in the consciousness of Their disciples the principles of certainty, permanency and changelessness. Once such principles are built within a person, he is a more dependable person and one who can be trusted for responsible labor.

Fanaticism is the result of a crystallized thoughtform built in the mental plane, when one fails to contact the Changeless One in himself and in the Universe. This is why fanaticism breeds fear and anger, and acts for a short time as the representative of permanency. Joy cannot exist where fanaticism scatters its seeds. Expansion of consciousness slowly disperses fanaticism and allows joy to flow in.

Where there is joy, there is also a sense of changelessness and permanency.

2. There is an increasing joy in your heart when you realize that your life is dedicated to the service of humanity. No one can take such a joy from you. Service for the Common Good is the source of a great joy. Service for the Common Good is based on uplifting people, expanding their consciousness, giving them direction, enlightening their minds, inspiring beauty in them, leading them to sacrificial service, bringing unity in their lives, building bridges in people and between people, leading them to freedom, and cultivating in them the sense of responsibility.

When you are convinced that you are doing a service for humanity, you will have a continuous joy within your heart. Even if people do not recognize your service, even if you are not paid for it, your service turns into a fountain of joy. You feel temporary joy in serving your family or your nation, but permanent joy comes to your heart when you start to serve in the name of humanity and for humanity.

There is partial joy and there is complete joy. Partial joy ends with sorrow; complete joy remains forever. Even individually, all that you are as a unit must absorb the joy — not one part of you. When one part of your body enjoys at the expense of the others, it leads to pain or sorrow.

3. Joy dawns in your heart when your life is not burdened by a heavy karma. If your life is loaded with memories of crimes, it will be very difficult for you to find the fountain of joy, even if you try to create it by artificial means. When you have in your mind memories of crimes, they short-circuit the electricity of your joy. No matter how hard you try to uplift yourself into the sphere of joy, something within you interferes. It disturbs your meditation, your singing, your dancing, and you feel that no matter what you do, you cannot sense a real joy.

The accumulated karma of various crimes builds a barrier between you and the source of joy, even if you do not remember the crimes. The elimination of karmic debt brings you joy. But if your consciousness has the memories of you hurting people, misleading people, exploiting people, manipulating people, stealing from people, lying to people, or slandering people, it will be very difficult for you to have joy. Such recordings will disturb the tranquility and serenity of your heart. When your heart is disturbed by your own wrong-doings, joy does not stay there.

Saintliness and purity are joy. Guilt and crime are sources of sadness.

4. When you have an awareness that the seeds of the flowers you planted are sprouting, flourishing and radiating fragrance and beauty, you have joy. You can expect a great harvest of joy when you plant in Space the seeds of beauty, goodness, justice, unity and freedom. Without these seeds, your future gardens will be barren, sandy and rocky.

How can one face eternity with joy, without having a great harvest from the seeds he planted in the hearts and lives of people? Your creative labor is the source of many seeds. You can throw seeds of beauty, light and love abundantly through your art, through your knowledge, through your sacrificial service, and you can have a great harvest of joy.

The seeds of beauty, goodness, justice, joy and freedom will bloom not only on this Earth, but in higher realms. Before you rise to these realms, your gardens will flourish and await your arrival. The results of the seeds of beauty travel faster than your actual evolution and attainments.

5. **At the moment when you meet upon any field of human endeavor your co-workers, who are dedicated to the upliftment of humanity, you have joy.** Do you have co-workers who have dedicated their lives for a great cause, who stand by you in darkness and in light, and who carry on the labor of beauty, goodness, justice, unity and freedom? It is a great privilege to have people around you to whom you can entrust your life, your plans, your purpose, your treasures, and all that you are. It is from such people that emerge those who are not only faithful to your goal, but are also prepared and ready to assist you in your field of labor to help you reach your goal.

Real co-workers are sources of joy. You know that they will consciously and intelligently help you in your labor, and they will even carry on your labor when you depart from them.

Great labor cannot be carried on alone. A great labor is a teamwork. This team is composed of co-workers who not only have the awareness of the goal, knowledge, skill, and endurance, but are also enthusiastic, self-sacrificing and highly dedicated to the goal. When one meets such co-workers, he feels a joy that is extremely rare.

6. **When a new and greater field of service is given to you, joy opens to you.** Whenever you are faithful to the field of labor, you are in joy and you do your best there.

The Watchful Eyes follow your steps, and when you are ready, they promote you to a greater field of service where you will have longer hours of work, heavier problems, greater demands of courage and daring, and deeper loneliness. But you will feel a tremendous kind of joy which will fill your entire being. Such a joy will be yours when you realize the honor and trust given to you, by granting to you a greater field of responsibility, in which you will be able to express your gratitude to the One Who is your Inner Essence.

New and more difficult fields of service stimulate deeper layers of your Core and evoke new creative energies. This is what the process of true self-actualization is. Many centers of our Core remain dormant for centuries until more daring fields of service challenge them and put them in action. The consciousness expands in recognizing and facing new fields of responsibility. When the sense of responsibility dulls, the downfall of an individual or a nation begins.

7. When you meet your Inner Watch, when you meet your Teacher and through your Inner Watch and Teacher you stand in the presence of Christ, you have joy. When you see Him, the joy that you will feel will be permanent, and "no man will be able to take that joy away."[1] The reason for such a joy is that in His image, you will see your own future perfection. You will be flooded with His joy of achievement and spiritual attainment.

There are various other physical ways that one may give joy to others:
1. By appreciating their beauty and their talents, and by promoting their creativity.
2. By giving proper gifts and meeting needs. Gifts can carry a great charge of joy to others.
3. By visiting your beloved ones, or those who are sick.
4. By writing letters of encouragement, affirmation or enlightenment.
5. By spreading hope, by speaking about the future, and by inspiring courage.

A joyful society is a healthy and prosperous society.

Why is joy so important and necessary for our lives?

1. Joy regenerates and rejuvenates your energy system and causes sublimation. In the future, people will apply joy to

---

[1] John XVI:22.

heal and uplift people. They will apply the joy of beauty, the joy of goodness, the joy of sacrifice, and the joy of creative art, and they will heal people. Joy is one of the greatest healing and energizing powers.

Joy not only heals, but also sublimates. Through joy your higher centers begin to be active and pump up the energies of the corresponding lower centers. It is in the light of joy that one shares and becomes selfless; his greed and ego vanish in the light of joy.

When I was a child my sister, who was five years older than I, had a very beautiful, colorful ball. She used to play with it, bouncing it on the ground and jumping over it, catching it in various ways, and then putting it in her pocket and running away. I also wanted to play with it, but she never wanted to give it to me.

One day, my uncle brought a horse for her. The horse was very beautiful. "Uncle," I said, "I will run and tell her about the horse!"

I ran half a mile. My sister was sitting under a huge oak tree. "Sister, Sister!" I screamed. "You have a horse! It is a gift for you!"

She began to jump in joy, and asked, "Where is it?"

"Uncle has it in front of the house."

She began to run. Suddenly she stopped. Taking the ball from her pocket, she said to me, "Take it," and she continued running.

I was in heaven. I had the ball which I never expected to have.... Years later, thinking about the event, I concluded that joy shares; joy makes people impersonal, beautiful and generous. It is in moments of joy that the deeper layers of "heart" come into manifestation.

2. **Joy clears away from your emotional and mental vehicles negative elements, destructive elements, and selfish elements.** The energy of joy purifies and expands your consciousness. Each moment of joy stays within your nature as a reservoir of energy for future use. Joyful people are more creative and

more productive, and they live longer. They spread health and happiness to their surroundings.

3. Joy increases your magnetism to higher thoughts, ideas, impressions and energies. The greatest moment of inspiration for new ideas, new visions, new plans and new breakthroughs is the moment when your heart is in joy.

4. Joy raises the power of your endurance and helps you to overcome many hindrances on the path of your labor. When you are joyful, you can work ten hours without a break and not feel tired or depressed. But when you start a job in complaint and negativity, you will soon feel tired.

Joy makes you assimilate prana. As certain vitamins cannot be assimilated without taking other elements with them, similarly the prana of higher spheres cannot be assimilated without joy. You even digest your food better when you are joyful. Prana energizes your system and makes you able to endure different conditions. As difficulties increase, joy supplies more energy to overcome them.

5. Joy makes your mind clear and your heart sensitive. The most sensitive moment of your life is the moment when you are in joy.

One day my father took me to a place where certain sacred dances were being performed. I was full of joy seeing the very colorful dresses and the intricate and subtle movements of the dancers' hands and feet, and hearing the extremely touching music. A moment came when I began to cry, in joy and in sadness.

Looking at my eyes, my father said, "You have tears of joy, but also I see sadness in your eyes.... Why?"

I brought my lips close to his ear and said, "I wish my sisters were here, too, to enjoy these dances."

Tears came to his eyes, and he hugged me.

When a pure joy touches your heart, you want to share it at least with those whom you love most, or with those who are deprived of it most. I noticed that even one's memory becomes brighter in the light of joy.

6. Joy charges your co-workers and makes them more efficient in their labor. A joyful leader can accomplish greater tasks than one who is always in self-pity. A joyful secretary produces more work than one who is stuck with her petty problems. A joyful person is like a dynamo who continuously imparts energy to the hearts of his co-workers.

7. Joy draws the attention of angelic hosts and the Great Ones. The emanations of joy enable the Invisible Ones to approach your sphere and directly communicate with you, inspire you and help you. Your joy convinces Them that you will not misuse Their treasures; you will not bury the "talents," but make good use of them.

The emanations of joy create a symphony of colors around your aura and a signal to angelic hosts. As one is attracted to a beautiful flower or a beautiful melody, in the same manner, supermundane "lotuses" are attracted to those who radiate the beauty of joy.

A great Teacher once said, "If only once you hear the songs We sing during Our labor, you will understand the depth of Our joy."[2]

---

[2]Excerpt from Chapter 30 of *Challenge for Discipleship*, by T. Saraydarian.

Joy And The Memory Of Home

Within each human being there is the "memory of Home." The memory of Home is a very beautiful memory, a feeling that once upon a time the Spark or the Spirit within our hearts was part of the Sun, was part of the omnipotent, omnipresent and omniscient Existence from which the Spark was projected out into Space as a Ray, and eventually was trapped in the world of matter, emotion and mind.

Home is total bliss or beatitude, the memory of which still remains in our hearts as the hope and path on which we will return Home. Thus each Spark of life has the urge to be happy, to be in joy and in bliss.

We feel that our present state is not the state in which we want to be. We do not have a state of permanent satisfaction, so we want something different, something more, and we do not yet clearly know for what it is we are searching. There is a faint memory of it, and in rare moments of happiness, joy and bliss, we feel we are approaching Home.

All that we want to do, all that we want to be in this world, is to be happy, to be full of joy, to be full of bliss, or to be bliss. All the rest are ways and means to reach the Source of our memory.

In the *Upanishads* it says, "Tat tvam asi." You are that; you are the supreme bliss in your Essence; your Self is part of that Life from which all things proceeded.

It is very interesting that, blinded by our ignorance and material life, we search for bliss in our physical happiness, in our emotional pleasures, in our plans and logic, in dollars, in possessions and positions, in diplomas, in our ranks and titles.... After searching for and attaining all that we want, we realize that the real joy and real bliss are not found in them ... and we ask, "Where can I find satisfaction for my thirsty heart?"

The answer is given to us by the sages of all ages: "Bliss is within you; bliss is you. Meet yourself, be yourself, and you will find the answers to your questions."

When our consciousness is focused within our physical, emotional or mental natures, we are always in fear. There are three main areas where our consciousness can be focused in the physical, emotional or mental realms:

1. Personality consciousness sees things as they appear. It is conditioned by death, disintegration, sickness, loss, loneliness, pain; by various needs; by the things you want to have and you do not have; by things you have but you lose. It is based on fear, greed, hatred, and anger.

Often our happiness is based upon a successful business, but we see that it does not last forever. Things happen and the business goes wrong. Many great businesses were destroyed by an earthquake, by an epidemic, by a hurricane, by the death of certain executives, by war or by revolution. Happiness based on things that are not permanent has always carried the seeds of sorrow and misery.

2. When we are identified with our emotional pleasures or emotional objects, we feel happy. But then we experience bitterness and pain when we lose our emotional objects with their pleasures. We eventually learn that there is no permanent happiness in our emotional objects, because they come and go with mixed pleasures and inherent sorrows. But the search continues. No matter how much disappointment life gives us, we keep searching for happiness until we gradually turn to a higher level of existence.

3. We begin to search for our happiness within the mental realms. Mental objects catch our attention because we see that there are more stability and permanency in the mental plane than on the previous two planes — the physical and emotional planes.

In the mental plane, some of us search for our happiness in daydreams, in religion, philosophy, or ideology, but eventually we find that these also do not give us the satisfaction or joy for which we were looking.

When we are identified with our thoughtforms, with our religion, philosophy, or ideology, we are always in a state of fear of losing them. Such a fear leads us into destructive actions in which are found the seeds of sorrow and pain. The destiny of fanatics of all ages is a witness to this fact.

A fanatic is a person who is identified with his religion or his racial or national superstitions, which eventually become a burden on his back and the source of his suffering.

There is also a tendency to search for joy and bliss in high positions or careers. It is possible to have temporary joy in mental objects and mental interests, but eventually we find out that it is possible to be a lawyer, but not necessarily a happy person; that it is possible to be a doctor, but not necessarily a healthy person; that it is possible to be a space scientist, but not necessarily a contented person; that it is possible to be the president of a great nation, but be loaded with heavy guilt feelings or frustrations.

The pursuit of happiness in all of these fields ends with disappointment. In the final analysis, we find that we had drops of joy only in those creative moments when we tried to serve, to uplift, and to bring joy to others during our search for happiness in our physical, emotional and mental objects.

I was talking with a heart surgeon when he was close to death. He said, "I am dying an unhappy man because all that I did was blindly motivated to collect thousands of dollars. I married a very beautiful woman who was the wife of my best friend; then I divorced her because I found a younger girl, and then she died in an accident. Now everything is ending in tragedy.... My wealth goes to my children, who dope themselves day and night."

There was only one thing I could say to him: "You will have more chances to search for your joy in the more permanent values of life in another cycle."

Our physical, emotional and mental happiness is intensified when we integrate our personality vehicles — our physical, emotional and mental natures — and enjoy our sunny days as a united mechanism. Thus our integrated personality is internally content, but is subject to those outside conditions which are related to our physical, emotional and mental life.

Man is like a boat on the ocean. He enjoys a few sunny days and then is caught by wind, rain or snow. Then he alternately passes through dark and sunny days. His happiness always has a short life.

When man's personality is healthy and in a state of satisfaction with what he has, with what he feels, and with what he knows and is, he feels an intense happiness. Many personalities were temporarily happy in the ocean of their physical possessions, emotional pleasures and mental interests. But when the storms came, they lost all that they had, because their treasure was carried away in the boat of the personality.

Happiness is related to the personality, and the first phase of the search for bliss is carried on in the field of personality, in which only a faint flash of happiness exists.

Buddha once said, "Everything is suffering — birth is suffering, life is suffering, death is suffering." The reason for this suffering is that man is identified with his physical, emotional and mental interests. One must pass through such experiences of dissatisfaction on the personality level before he starts to search for bliss somewhere else. The disappointment of the personality as a whole causes a new breakthrough into a new dimension.

I knew an extremely beautiful twenty-one-year-old girl, whom I had not seen for twenty years. One day a middle-aged woman visited me and asked, "Do you know me?"

I answered, "Your eyes are familiar, but I do not remember where we met or what your name is."

She looked like a witch; her face was wrinkled, her eyes were blackened, her hair was in a desperate condition, and she smelled heavily of liquor. She said, "I am very unhappy. Don't you remember me? I am B...."

"I can't believe my eyes."

"Yeah," she said, "I am ugly, right?"

"My goodness!"

She fell into my arms and began to cry.

"What happened to you? Why didn't you contact me?"

"I don't know. I want to die."

"Why?"

"Because I lost my beauty, and because I lost my beauty, I lost my friends; because I lost my friends, I lost my job."

"You can be beautiful again."

"With such a face?"

"Beauty is not in our face or in our body; beauty is in our hearts and souls, in our ideas and dreams, in our sacrificial service, in Christ. You can be beautiful again if you look for it — not in your personality, but in your soul. When the soul shines, even the rocks radiate beauty."

"Can I find my happiness again?"

"You don't need to be happy; you need to be joyful."

"Joyful?"

"Yes, joyful. To find joy you will search not in the places where you were looking, but beyond your personality — in your *Inner Core*."

"You never changed," she noticed. "How come you do not hate me in this shape?"

"You are always beautiful, and because you are now disappointed, a new path is opening in front of you."

No one can really advance in a higher search if the foundation on which he stands is not shaken and destroyed. You need a crisis to make a breakthrough. The wind and the storm must come and hit your existence, and test your foundation. Is your foundation based on your bank account, on your present health, on your position, on your friends? All of these can be taken from you in one storm if your foundation is not built on your spiritual achievements and realizations. If your foundation is built on the solid rock of the Transpersonal Self within you, no power can destroy it. Only in Soul-awareness do you taste the beauty of joy.

First you were a boat; now you are a spaceship soaring into Space, free from the destructive effects of waves, storms, lightning, clouds and earthquakes.

A conscious soul is an indestructible beauty and joy. Thus, the next stage in the search for bliss is Soul-consciousness. This is the stage in which joy starts. You are in the Soul, and your realization is different. Instead of being subjected to fear, anger, hatred, and greed, you are in the domain of a new consciousness, the main characteristics of which are:

>Love
>Immortality
>Service
>Joy
>Contact with the Hierarchical Plan
>Creativity

Love is the ability to identify oneself with the life-aspect of manifestation.

Immortality is the realization that one was, one is, and one will always be an individual existence. Immortality cannot be taught; it must be experienced. It is the result of spiritual achievement.

A characteristic of the Transpersonal Self is love, a love that is given without expectation and anticipation. As you give more love, you have more joy. Expectation relates you to personality levels.

Service is the ability to put into all of your activities the solar fire of love and the fire of the Plan. The Plan can be contacted in the Soul levels. It is an experience, not a teaching. The Plan is the map which shows you how to return to the Sun from which you were radiated out. The Plan is the map which shows you how to release yourself from the trap of your physical, emotional and mental bodies, and achieve the state of awareness which you had originally.

All human endeavors are efforts to escape the prisons that we built, or the prisons that others built for us. All human labor is the effort to escape the conditions which we hate. The Plan shows the way out of our prisons.

Service is the ability to express the fire of the Plan through all that we think, feel, speak and do.

In Soul-consciousness, we have the first experience of true joy. Joy is the realization that you are no longer vulnerable, that you can lose nothing, that greater achievements are waiting for you, that you can lift people to the level of Soul-consciousness where they taste the true joy, that now you can see things as they are — not as they appear to be.

Unless we achieve Soul-consciousness, we cannot understand the true meaning of invulnerability.

"Weapons cannot hurt the Self, nor fire burn It. Water cannot drench It, nor can wind make It dry. It cannot be divided. It is eternal and all-pervading."[1] Such an experience can be achieved in Soul-consciousness. As you go deeper into joy, you come closer to yourself. In joy, you have the realization that you can lose nothing.

In school we had a very beautiful teacher, who had the habit of taking his gold watch out of his pocket and putting it on the table. One day he came in and asked whether anyone had seen his watch. The students said, "No." He was my favorite teacher, and I felt angry that anyone would take his watch. I went to him and said, "Who do you think may have stolen it from you?"

"It is not stolen," he said.

"Then," I asked, "what happened to it?"

"Somebody is using it."

I could not understand the secret of his behavior; he always had a great flow of joy in all of his expressions. He was a joyful person.

In this event, my teacher gave me a chance to glimpse that in a certain state of consciousness you do not lose anything, because in Soul-consciousness, you do not possess anything.

---

[1]*The Bhagavad Gita,* translated by H. (Torkom) Saraydarian, Chapter II, Verses 23-24.

Once Christ said, "Do not be afraid of those who try to kill your body, but of those who try to kill your soul." Do not be afraid of those who try to attack your shadow, but be cautious of those who try to destroy your spiritual principles, your visions, your virtues, your values.

Joy gives a person the realization that greater achievements are waiting for him in the future. The vision of the future is an ever-growing joy in our hearts.

In Soul-consciousness, no matter through what your personality life is passing, there is a tomorrow, there is a new dawn, because the Soul is not limited by the failures of time, space and matter. Even the failures of the personality can be utilized as firewood for the bonfire of the Soul.

The greatest failure of a person is contained in his actions that are directed against the Law of Love.

Joy offers a person the innate conviction that he can lift someone to the level of joy, and make him joyful.

Once I was helping a young boy who was using drugs heavily. Eventually the boy overcame his habit, took up running, and began to study and to work. After being convinced that this was a permanent change in his being, I felt great joy. I went to my private room and asked myself, "Why are you so joyful?" "Oh my, a great burden is gone from my shoulders." "What burden?" "The burden of the usage of drugs."

Every time we help someone, we help ourselves. In Soul-consciousness, the fragrance of joy radiates when you engage yourself in a labor of helping others without expectation.

In Soul-consciousness, you have the eye to see things as they are, and not as they appear to be. When a person takes appearances as reality, he is caught in change. Joy is changelessness — in change.

It is told that the Law of Change is ever-ruling. This is true for the world of phenomena, but it is not true for the world of Spirit. We lose our state of changelessness and are caught in the changing phenomena of life as we identify ourselves with the vehicles of our personality.

In Soul-consciousness, man comes in contact with the plan of his life, and eventually penetrates into the Plan of the Hierarchy for humanity. It is very interesting to note that the plan of our life is found in our Soul, and the Plan for humanity is found in the Hierarchy. In having a contact with the Plan, a person becomes a co-worker of Great Servers of the human race. The Plan is formulated in such a way that It works for the welfare of humanity and for the welfare of each human being.

A Soul-conscious person tries to bring the Plan into daily life to help everyone, in every way, in everything, so that he is able to lead people from personality prisons to Soul-freedom, where they can experience joy.

The next characteristic of the Soul is creativity. There is a great joy in creativity, because creativity is the process of letting the energies of the Plan flow and nourish the Sparks of Infinity in each living form.

In the presence of really joyful persons, other people bloom. Joy is energy, and this energy nourishes the higher centers of human beings with the substance of higher mental fire. Then the hidden seeds of goodness, beauty and truth come to life in them.

Joy does not stimulate the lower centers because it has a special, high frequency which cannot be picked up by the lower centers. Joy does not over-stimulate lower centers.

After a person proves that he can live in joy and be an embodiment and a fountain of joy, he is allowed to penetrate into the sphere in which bliss and ecstasy are found. This sphere in esoteric terminology is called the Spiritual Triad.

Once I heard that there was a man in the Far East who was an advanced human being. I had a great desire to see him. When I finally located his place of retreat, his students told me that I could not see him because he was in meditation. I pretended that I was not interested in seeing him any more, but I found a way to go to his room, where he was sitting in meditation. He was in ecstasy. There was a peace in his room which you could almost touch. His face was radiating light and beauty.

I went a little closer, and I felt a fiery energy on my skin. It was a burning joy. I went closer and closer, until I sat by him. A few minutes later, my eyes closed and I was nowhere. I only felt a great joy, bliss and at-one-ment with all that exists. When later my consciousness returned to its normal level, I said to myself, "This is bliss. It is a state of awareness in which you transcend time, space and matter."

After anchoring myself on the mental plane, I slowly went again into the blissful state, in which I received unverbalized directions. I do not know how long I was in that state. I felt an arm around my shoulder and neck. I opened my eyes, and looked into his eyes. For the first time in my life, I saw Infinity. His eyes were doors leading to Infinity.

He did not talk; he hugged me and gave me a big smile. I went toward the door facing him, continuously looking at him.

In the Spiritual Triad, we contact bliss. And it is from bliss that beauty radiates.

The Spiritual Triad is the domain of Infinity where there is synthesis, there is Purpose, there is Will.

There are seven enemies of joy:

The first enemy is any action which causes or generates fear in other persons. Where there is fear, the bird of joy flies away.

The second enemy of joy is anger. Any time you act in anger, it deprives you of your joy. Anything you do to make others angry takes the real joy of life from your heart. Anger may satisfy your emotions, but not your heart.

The third enemy of joy is greed. Whenever you have greed in your heart, you lack joy. Greed is symbolized by a bottomless grave which never can be filled with human corpses. The most unhappy people are greedy people. Their happy moments are secured only by money, objects, liquor, or by short moments of pleasure. Even in those moments of pleasure, they feel the fear of losing their happiness. I have seen many families fall apart because of the greed of the father, who was so occupied in making money that he would almost forget that he had a family.

The fourth enemy of joy is hatred. Any person who has hatred in his heart, or any group or nation which is polluted by hatred, will never taste the sunshine of joy, neither in the present nor in the future.

Joy is the connecting consciousness which makes you realize that you are one with everything. Hatred is the feeling of separativeness. With hatred, you cut many electrical lines within your system and within the system of international relations, and when you turn off the switch of joy you have neither joy nor light. It is very interesting to notice that in joy, your light increases; you have purer discrimination and a better sense of values. In hatred, your light decreases and your sense of altruistic values is almost nil.

Let us remember that actions performed in fear, anger, hatred and greed, create much bad karma on our path.

In Soul-consciousness there is love. Love purifies you and leads you into the fiery sphere of the Spiritual Triad. In the awareness of that fiery sphere, you taste the mighty bliss which you had when you were still one with the undivided Space. That bliss was an unconscious bliss, and now your labor is to reach that bliss with your own effort and in your own right.

The fifth enemy of joy is ugliness. Once I was visiting a family and the father brought a birthday gift to his six-year-old child. It was a creature with a square head with horns, one eye looking east, the other eye looking west, ears hanging like bananas, legs tall and skinny like dry branches, one arm fat, one bony. It was an embodiment of real ugliness.

"Hey," I exclaimed, "don't give that ugly creature to your boy; it will distort his imagination. Get rid of that ugliness." Why couldn't he bring something beautiful, something that would inspire the boy and give him joy?

Once a movie producer said to me that criminal movies bring in more money than any other kind of film. "Yes," I told him, "they may do so, but where will you hide when crime increases around you?"

"Until then," he answered, "I will have plenty of money to go somewhere else!"

Ugliness brings money, but not joy.

When the producer was ready to leave in his car, he loaded a gun and sat on it. "My goodness," I thought, "he is in fear already."

The sixth enemy of joy is any action that is not based on goodwill. Such an action takes your joy away from you.

The seventh enemy of joy is any action that is not based on truth. Lies take away your joy.

Ultimately, joy is truth, beauty and goodness. It is the ability to stand within Soul-consciousness.

How can we climb to that level of Soul-consciousness?

1. **Through meditation on virtues.** In meditation, we withdraw ourselves from fear, hatred, greed and anger, and from their consequences and connections, and we stand in the light of our Inner Guide.

2. **Through causal thinking,** because it liberates us from being caught in the phenomenal world. Causal thinking is the ability to penetrate into the roots of events or find the originating cause, instead of being stuck in the results and effects.

3. **Through living a life of beauty in all of our expressions.** A great sage, speaking about joy, says, "It is useful to impregnate space with joy.... Joy is the health of the spirit."[2]

The first step toward joy is scientific meditation, through which you eventually achieve Soul-infusion. Scientific meditation is an effort to penetrate into the mind of the real Thinker, which is the Soul. This is the Transpersonal Self, or the Inner Guide.

In scientific meditation you begin to control, to discipline, and to clear your mind so that it totally obeys your commands and does not become a victim of the thoughts or suggestions coming from other minds.

---

[2]Agni Yoga Society, *Fiery World*, Vol. I, para. 298.

There is a serious sickness in the world, which we can call "abandonment of the boat." People allow other people to use their mental "boat" through hypnotism, suggestions, force, and other influences. As long as our minds do not belong to us, we cannot think — and if we cannot think, those people who think through us will control us.

The Teaching tells us that we must not allow other minds to rule our minds. We must use our own minds and learn how to think. Meditation is the first step toward that freedom.

Joy abides with those who know how to think. Real thinking leads us to freedom. Real thinking is the only means to escape imprisonment of the Spirit in any form. Thus on the path of joy, we learn how to think, how to meditate.

Self-actualization cannot be achieved when other people use your mind. Your mind is your steering wheel. When other people have control over your steering mechanism, you have no way of knowing where they are leading you.

The second step toward joy is questioning. Daily events, national events and international events do not exist without causes. Ask yourself the reasons why these events took place. Develop observation of the causes. Try to see the cause behind every event. This will reveal to you many laws, principles, motives and intentions hidden behind many relationships and activities. Understanding the causes will help you to direct your steps goal-fittingly.

Try to consider the cause, not the manifestation. Do not react to the effects, but to the causes whenever possible. Self-deception descends on us when we occupy ourselves with the phenomena and forget about causes or the reasons why.

When you continue searching for the cause of events, you will eventually develop "double-leveled" sight, which reads the lines, and also reads between the lines of the events.

The third step is to live a life of beauty in our personality, home, speech, manners, behavior, relationships, emotional responses, thoughts, ideas, visions and expressions. As we express beauty, the fire of joy increases in our vehicles and radiates out, warming the hearts of others. True joy manifests through beauty because joy is the expression of the Soul. Bliss is the expression of the Self.

Joy opens people's hearts; they talk and confess to you when they see there is abundant joy within you. Joy builds communication lines, gives strength and leads you to success. Any labor started and continued in joy will be a successful labor.

Joy never threatens people. They feel safe in the presence of a joyful person because a joyful person is above personality interests. His nature is love.

Try joyfully to release, joyfully to resign and detach, joyfully to pay your bills. Joyfully renounce and joyfully live if you want your life to be a blessing for the world.

A great sage, speaking about joy, says:

> [A]byssees have been crossed through joy and trust. Not only courage, but precisely joy makes you invulnerable.[3]

Also:

> The manifestation of joy is accompanied by intensification of the work of the centers. Many attainments are accomplished by the manifestation of joy.[4]

Fear creates doubt. Doubt wastes energy. Joy annihilates fear.

Joy increases our daring. One is daring when there is no fear in his heart.

Psychologically dark moments of life can be crossed only through joy. Joy keeps your engine running. Joy gives clarity of vision to your mind. Fear, depression and doubt poison the blood and the brain, and the mind cannot see things as they are. A poisoned bloodstream is the cause of most of our failures and ill-judgment.

---

[3] Agni Yoga Society, *Fiery World*, Vol. II, para. 110.
[4] Agni Yoga Society, *Agni Yoga*, para. 459.

Joy creates radioactivity in the aura, which repels all unworthy thoughts and negative emotions, and builds a shield around the body. A joyful heart cannot be wounded by the flying arrows of the dark forces.

The etheric centers are intensified by joy, because joy is the fire of the Soul, and its flame creates radioactivity in the centers and synchronizes their rhythms. Thus, higher joy expands the fiery spheres of higher centers, which puts the consciousness of man in contact with higher planes. These are the moments of new realizations and new insights. New achievements are accomplished because of such contact and insight.

The flame of joy is the fire which emanates from the center of the Chalice, from the center of the twelve-petaled Lotus in the higher mind. It is this flame which leads the steps of man to the Innermost Sanctuary — Home.[5]

---

[5] Taken from Chapter 10-II of ***The Flame of Beauty, Culture, Love, Joy***, by T. Saraydarian.

Love
And Joy

*T*here are three basic energies which, when used intelligently, make a person healthy, wealthy and creative. These three energies are light, love, and will. Light and will combined produce joy. Every time your light and your will power increase, you enter into a greater joy.

An enlightened person is always in continuous joy, because at the time of real enlightenment he comes in contact with the energy of will power within his nature, and the will aspect begins to control. Enlightenment expands the horizon of joy; will power gives stability to joy. A joyful person radiates. All his actions on any level are creative, because the roots of his actions are extended into the realm of joy.

Joy combined with love produces the energy of healing and the energy of attraction. In the presence of a loving and joyful person, creative possibilities bloom in your heart. You become magnetic and attract all those who will work for you and for their own success. Your love and joy inspire them and charge them, and they give their utmost to increase the source of their joy and love. People search for joy and love, and when they find them, nothing can prevent sacrificing all that is necessary to support that source of love and joy.

Love is our Essence. When we love, we release our Essence. "To live" means to bring your Essence into expression, into release. The only time that we really live is the time that we love, when our Inner Essence is in manifestation. The measure of our life is the measure of our love. You live as long as you love. If you "lived" ninety-five years, but loved only one year, you did not live for ninety-five years, but for only one year — not more. The rest was a waste of time. You can actually write on the tombstone of such a person:

> "Here lies Mr. So-and-So.
> He was born in 1885
> and passed away in 1980
> but he lived only one year."

People will be surprised, but never mind, for they will eventually realize that a life lived for one's own sake does not count. It is only a life lived for the service of others that counts. Such a life of service is a life of love and joy.

In loving, you release your Essential Self — the condensed and individualized life. Life is creative. It not only manifests through creative thoughts, feelings and actions, but also makes others creative and radioactive.

In every act of real love and real joy, you are manifesting your Inner Core. When your Essence is in operation, in expression, you are alive. You are alive when you express love.

Joy and love operate through our five senses on the physical, emotional and mental planes. When the energy of joy and love operates through our five senses on the physical plane, it creates a happy person. Through all his senses, such a person enjoys the Universe. His senses operate at their maximum capacity and transmit to him the thrill of the objective world.

It is your love and joy that transform the world, as you contact it with your five senses. Nothing seems pleasant and delightful if the energy of love and joy does not flow through your senses and come in contact with the world of the five senses. Whatever you hear, touch, see, taste and smell, transmits your pleasure and happiness when you are full of love and joy.

The energy of love and joy on the emotional plane creates aspiration, ecstasy, fiery devotion, and one-pointedness toward higher values.

In the mental plane, the energy of love and joy creates greater vision, creative striving, understanding, insight, foresight, synthetic perception and creativity. Love and joy give power to your mind to penetrate into greater mysteries of higher contact and the ability to sustain your freedom in all your contacts.

The problems of the world can be solved by the energy of love and joy. Bring love and joy into the meetings at the United Nations, and the problems of the world will lose their control and gradually melt away.

Love and joy operate on higher planes, too. For example, on the Intuitional Plane, love and joy create revelation. When you touch the network of causes and blueprints, then all outer events are simplified in your loving and joy-radiating vision.

In the Atmic Plane, the energy of love and joy turns into the power of will, enthusiasm, fearlessness and command.

In the Monadic Plane, love unifies the person with the "solar whole," and joy pours down as creative energy, purifying, energizing, enlightening and impressing with the Divine Beauty of higher realms.

On the Divine Plane, joy becomes a door through which flames of light, love and power pass to Cosmic dimensions.

Love and joy are the foundations of any creative and progressive work. There is no real and true joy if that joy is not imbued with love. Love cannot exist without joy.

The energy of love and joy:
1. heals,
2. harmonizes,
3. expands,
4. creates magnetism,
5. reveals,
6. uplifts, and
7. strengthens.

1. Love and joy heal. They heal physical, emotional and mental wounds and sicknesses, align and integrate the physical and etheric centers, and purify the astral body, building the way of sublimation for the sacral and solar plexus centers.

Emotional attachment, low-level desires, glamour and negative emotions, are slowly washed away by the increasing energy of joy and love. If one exercises joy and love for half an hour daily, he will be a new person in a very short time.

The energy of love and joy has a great effect on mental health. In a loving and joyful atmosphere, the mind gets sharper, clearer, with increasing power of insight and foresight. Love links a person with the realm of intuition. Joy builds the bridge toward Higher Worlds.

2. Love and joy have a great harmonizing effect on our physical, emotional and mental nature. They create harmony in groups, and raise their efficiency. They create harmony in nations and in humanity. Love and joy link humanity with greater centers of wisdom, light and power.

Love and joy affect animals, and make them more protective of their masters, and more productive.

Love and joy affect the plant kingdom — trees, bushes, flowers and vegetables. Give love and joy, and your aura will nourish the vegetable kingdom; your trees will bear more fruit, and your flowers will be more fragrant.

3. Love and joy are energies which cause expansion. They expand your consciousness, your horizon, and your inclusiveness. They expand the field of your spiritual influence.

Art uplifts and transforms people when it is charged with the energy of love and joy. A joyful expression of creative talent expands the understanding of people. An artwork full of love makes people touch higher dimensions.

4. Love and joy charge the etheric, astral and mental bodies with magnetism. Man's personality becomes a magnet, attracting higher ideas and visions, as well as prana from the sun. The real assimilation of prana and food is at its highest when a person loves and is full of joy. Loving and joyful persons attract those who help them and support their service for humanity.

A joyful and loving person lives in abundance, enjoying the fruits of his labor. Many people make money, but they do not enjoy it until love and joy fill their hearts.

5. **Love and joy slowly remove the veils, walls and hindrances between people, and establish contact and communion.** People reveal themselves when they feel that you love them, when they feel that you have joy in your heart. Love and joy create great trust and allow you to see things in people you have never seen. Through love and joy, the causes of problems are seen and handled in the right way. Love removes barriers existing between people. Joy removes barriers between planes.

6. **Joy and love uplift people.** As we increase our love and joy step by step, we raise the focus of our consciousness, we raise our social status, we raise our love, we uplift our hearts and our minds from the petty problems of life, and we fill our hearts with inspiration for our future achievements.

Extend your hand with joy and love, and people will grasp it and lift themselves up from their common troubles and anxieties. Approach the sick with love and joy, and their tonality will change and rise. Speak with joy and love, and you will uplift the masses.

7. **Joy is a tonic for the nerves; love purifies the blood and strengthens the heart.** Joy and love are great shields against psychic attacks and against dark forces. Negative and dark forces hate joy, and they cannot breathe in the fragrance of love.

Love and joy strengthen a group, a society, a nation, and make them invincible.

Before you eat or drink anything, charge your food or water with love and joy, and you will notice a great difference in your health. Before you speak, before you try to serve, charge yourself with love and joy, and you will see how people are elevated and strengthened.

The radiation of love reveals greater depths of your nature. With these greater depths, greater joy flows out. As you love, you reveal your Innermost Essence. Through your own Essence, the Essence of the Great Mystery dawns in your heart.

Love and joy are carriers of the Divine Purpose. "God is Love." In loving, you will meet God. Without love, one will never understand the Plan and Purpose of God.

To understand love and joy, we must try to experience them. Any time we love, we must try to know the level of our love and its motive. It may be physical love, emotional love, mental love or higher love. It can be personal love, group love, national love, global love, or a love for Infinity.

As the level of love rises and the motive behind it becomes more inclusive, your consciousness expands and your understanding deepens in the same degree.

The same thing must be done with our joy. See where your joy lies, where it starts and where it ends. Find the causes of your joy, and try to clearly see the level where it originated.

After seeing a few levels of your joy, try to raise the level of your joy and make it more inclusive, to the point where you feel joy for the whole existence. After such a stage of joy, you become a flow of love and joy.

The energy of love and joy can manifest on any level of human existence. As the level through which the energy of love and joy expresses itself is raised, you receive a deeper and better response from the world. Your deeper joy evokes a deeper joy from others. Your deeper love evokes a deeper love from others. Eventually, one reaches a stage where love and joy fuse with the love and joy of millions. This fusion opens the gates of the future for humanity and protects humanity from wrong or self-destructive actions.

> *... The measure of understanding is the degree of love ... love above all attracts the Fire of Space.... [A]s a lever sets the wheels in motion, so love sets up the strongest reaction. Compared with the radiance of love, the strongest hatred reflects only as a hideous mark. For love is the true reality and treasure.*[1]

---

[1] Agni Yoga Society, *Agni Yoga*, para. 424.

"The measure of understanding is the degree of love ... love above all attracts the Fire of Space...." The Fire of Space is the love contained in the space in which we live, move and have our being. When you keep loving, your love increases, raising its level to such a degree that eventually you become a total sacrifice for humanity. The Fire of Space consumes you. The fire of love consumes you. Nothing remains in you except love — a total love for life and all its forms.

The Fire of Space consumes all that is attached to you, but you are not annihilated. You, as a drop, become the ocean. Just one second of realization of this blessed state takes away all fear, and you shine with the love of life.

"[A]s a lever sets the wheels in motion, so love sets up the strongest reaction." Your love deepens and increases as the reaction to your love increases. Ingratitude, betrayals of various forms, hatred, and action taken to destroy your reputation and labor are reactions to your love. Because of your love, these strong reactions open the way of your love's ray to pour out abundantly. Eventually, reaction turns into a response.

Love and joy work miracles in those conditions where there is a lack of love and joy. That is why the enemy must be respected, because he freely works for your improvement and perfection.

"Compared with the radiance of love, the strongest hatred reflects only as a hideous mark. For love is the true reality and treasure." The radiance of love increases as you love more. Love, if used continuously on one level without trying to use it on higher levels, eventually becomes your enemy, and burns your mechanism. The safest way to use love energy is to continuously make efforts to use it on higher and higher levels and planes as the need arises.

If a person has one level of love and there is no striving to raise this level, you get tired of that person and look for one who can love with you on many levels and planes — or on all planes, if necessary. If love does not increase, it decreases and turns into a negative force. Love only exists in its process of expansion. Decreasing love turns into hatred, into self-interest, into "mine and yours," into anger, violence, jealousy, and eventually apathy and inertia.

> ... Two thousand years ago it was pointed out that Fire would devour the Earth. Many thousands of years ago the Patriarchs warned humanity of the fiery peril. Science has failed to pay attention to many signs. No one is willing to think on a planetary scale. Thus We speak before the awesome time. One may still not escape the last hour. Help can be extended, but hatred will not be a healer.[2]

The "awesome time" is in front of us. It is the time of atomic war, of natural cataclysm, of depression, of hatred, of unemployment, and of the degeneration of morals. It is the time of the increase of crime, drug abuse, pollution, and so on. When the results of all of these are combined, you have the "awesome time" — the Armageddon of the seers.

Scientists have kept themselves busy flooding the market with their inventions, but they have given little attention to the increasing pollution belt around the planet. We are told that this five- to ten-mile accumulation of gases can one day ignite and catch on fire, and the planet with all of its scientists can burn to ashes. No one will be saved if this madness of playing with Nature continues.

Before that awesome hour, it is possible to change the direction of life through love and joy, which will lead the planet into sanity, health, purity and beauty. To work for the welfare of one humanity, we must check our lives and see if there is an increasing joy and love behind all that we think, feel and do.

One day a lawyer friend told me, "I worked day and night and became a money machine. There is no love or joy in such a mechanical life."

I told him that there were millions of people like him, and the only way to escape such a mechanical life was to introduce joy

---

[2]Agni Yoga Society, *Fiery World*, Vol. II, para. 9.

into all his thoughts, feelings and actions, and start doing things as a loving service for others.

We know that the planet and humanity can be saved by the heroic efforts of those who love this planet and who love humanity.

> ... *No creative attainment, no cooperation, in fact no community is possible without magnanimity. One can observe how through magnanimity labor is made tenfold easier and, it would seem, nothing could be simpler during an inspired work than to wish only for the good and for success of one's neighbor! Joy is the result of manifested labor. Joy is a great helper.*[3]

Labor is striving to change the life and make the planet a better place to live. Labor is striving to make people love more, to make their love inclusive. Through such a labor, joy is released and manifested. Joy inspires you to carry on your labor in spite of all adverse conditions. Each true labor increases your joy, and joy increases your enthusiasm to labor more.

Magnanimity is the ability to stand above all adverse conditions in great love and joy. It is the ability to carry on your labor with vision and with the inspiration of the Future. Magnanimity is a great spiritual solemnity and dignity of the Spirit. It is the royal grandeur of the Inner, Divine Self. It is magnanimity that radiates the solemn joy, the profound love that persists in all adverse conditions.

> *Joy lies within itself and has first of all, the quality of directness, straight-forwardness and a smile for everything. Precisely joy helps to bridge over all hostile obstacles. Joy is one of the best means for the overcoming of hostile attacks.... Joy is always the shortest path to exaltation....*[4]

---

[3] Agni Yoga Society, *Fiery World*, Vol. III, para. 424.
[4] Roerich, Nicholas K., *Abode of Light*, p. 41.

This is so beautiful. One can use the above quotation for a year as a seed thought for meditation. Great sages advised their students to meditate on joy and measure their daily life by the standards of joy. Exaltation of the human spirit can be seen only in a joy flaming with love. Joy transforms our being and lifts us closer to our Essence.

> *Speaking of the kinds of love, let us note the love that holds back and the love that inspires. In essence the first love is earthly, and the second is heavenly. But what a multitude of constructive efforts were destroyed by the first! And a similar multitude winged by the second! The first is aware of all the limitations of space and consciousness; but the second has no need of earthly measurements.... [T]he second love embraces the physical world and the Subtle and Fiery Worlds as well. It kindles hearts for the highest joy and is thus indestructible. Thus, let us expand the heart — not for Earth but for Infinity.*[5]

People "expand the heart" for the Earth to possess the Earth, and eventually find out that they are possessed by the Earth. Thus, joy disappears. Thus, love disappears. The Earth absorbs them.

When people expand their hearts toward Infinity or spiritual values, the Earth Itself offers Its beauty and love, and helps people to climb toward their true destination. We are told that owning the Earth is not our destination. Earth is a station along the path toward Infinity. Those who are possessed by the Earth will remain with It, as a passenger dropped off the train.

> *... It is useful to impregnate space with joy, and very dangerous to strew the heavens with sorrow.... Joy is the health of the spirit.*[6]

---

[5] Agni Yoga Society, **Heart**, para. 242.
[6] Agni Yoga Society, **Fiery World**, Vol. I, para. 298.

"It is useful to impregnate space with joy." We seldom realize that as we think, feel and act, we inject various kinds of substance into Space. Joy is a substance; fear is another substance. Love, hatred and gratitude are different kinds of substances. It is necessary to ask ourselves what kind of substance we are dumping into Space.

Space can be polluted with the substance of illusions, glamours and wrong motives. Such substances contaminate people who, because of their various weaknesses, draw these substances into their mechanisms.

It is also important to know that each human being has a space, a sphere around his body. This sphere can expand or contract. It expands if the substance you are injecting into the greater Space is in the nature of love, joy and beauty. But if the substance you are injecting is in the nature of hatred, base thoughts and crimes, then you gradually narrow your space and bury yourself in your own negative and deadly substance. Many sicknesses of the mind, heart and body are the result of a narrowing sphere around you.

As your sphere expands through right thoughts, right action and loving conditions, through joy and love, you penetrate into greater Space and draw much finer living energy, light, love and power into your system.

The substance of joy is a great nourishment and a great tonic and inspiration for those who are striving on the path of service, on the path of enlightenment, and on the path of conscious evolution.

Our aura, impregnated with joy, is a colorful symphony with great magnetism. We often impregnate our rooms, our gardens and our offices with worries, with negative feelings, with destructive thoughtforms of various kinds. The sphere around our dwelling and working places gets so contaminated with such pollution that our soul has a hard time to breathe and to be creative. Instead of such negative substances, we can fill our homes and offices with the substance of joy and love, and thus increase our vitality, creativity and service for the world.

There was a depressed girl who worked in the post office near my home. She looked very sad. One day, instead of talking to her, I looked at her and smiled.

"What do you want?" she asked.

"Stamps."

"How many and what kind?"

"Three ten-cent stamps." I paid for the stamps, and said to her, "You know, your eyes ... oh, never mind."

"What about my eyes?"

"Your eyes...."

"Come on, what is it?"

"I can't tell you now...." and I left.

The next week, I waited until my turn came. She was looking and waiting for me.

"Two ten-cent stamps, please."

"What about my eyes?"

"You know, I want to tell you a secret."

"What is it?"

"When you smile, your eyes are so beautiful, but if you keep looking sad, your eyes look like the eyes of a witch."

"Is it really so?"

"Yes. Try always to smile and you will be so beautiful." She gave me a big smile and I departed.

Every time after that she gave me a bigger smile. Five months later, she disappeared. I asked another clerk, "Where is she?"

"Your smiling girl?"

"Yes."

"She was promoted. She is working in the office. You changed her life."

"May I see her?"

"Yes."

He went to inform her. She came out and hugged me, and with a most beautiful smile said, "The day you taught me to smile, a joy sprang out of my heart. I am happy now. Thank you for what you did for me."

Let us "impregnate space with joy." Start with a smile, and the rest will slowly follow.

"[It is] very dangerous to strew the heavens with sorrow.... Joy is the health of the spirit." A space stratified with sorrow is space through which destructive and negative forces operate. Even germs like a space full of sorrow; they grow there more abundantly. Dark forces like depression and sorrow, because they can easily control a person caught by sorrow and depression. Sorrow blocks the vision of the future, devitalizes your body and paralyzes your intellect.

> *... The successful mastery of all trials lies within our hearts and consists in our love for the Lord. If we are filled with love, can obstacles exist? Earthly love itself creates miracles. Does not the fiery love for Hierarchy multiply our forces?*[7]

We are told that the disciples came to Christ and said, "How will they know that we are Your disciples?" They were waiting for Him to say, "You will be a colonel. You will be a king. You will be a queen, and people will know that you are...." He answered, "The world will know that you are My disciples when you love each other." I believe He meant to say, "If you really love each other and do not let that love go, making that love deeper and deeper, they will know that you are My disciples, because I am Manifested Love. You can witness love only by being love. People will know if you are expressing, living or manifesting the substance — the love — that I brought you. But if you hate each other, if you create separativeness, you are not My disciples!"

---

[7] *Ibid.*, para. 637.

The greatest love and joy exist among those people who really serve the Lord and the Hierarchy. Their love is permanent, and their joy ever increases.

Striving toward the Lord pulls the human soul out of personality problems and relationships, and raises him closer to the Core of the Spirit. The closer one goes to his True Self, the greater are the radiations of joy and love.

Man charges himself with energy when he dedicates his life to an ideal.

> *It is said, "Do not enter Fire in inflammable garments, but bring a fiery joy." In this indication lies the entire prerequisite for communion with the Fiery World. Verily, even the garments of the Subtle World are not always suitable for the Fiery World. So, too, the joy of ascent must transcend any earthly joy.... Even in the flowers of Earth, in the plumage of birds, and in the wonders of the heavens, one can find that very joy which prepares one for the gates of the Fiery World.*[8]

"Inflammable garments" are the physical, emotional and mental vehicles which are full of pollutants of various kinds. Increasing energy from higher spheres burns your vehicles if they are not pure. Only a purified vehicle can withstand the pressure and the fire of the higher planes.

Fiery joy purifies the vehicles and makes them "fireproof." Fiery joy eliminates the vices of your bodies. Once they are purified from earthbound tendencies, they turn into channels of pure love, beauty, goodness and truth. It is only by purified "garments" that one can stand in the presence of a Great One, or enter His Ashram.

Love and joy increase on each step of our ascent toward the Lord, toward the vision. Only a life dedicated to human welfare witnesses the joy of ascent. Joy and love increase in our hearts to

---

[8]*Ibid.*, para. 638.

such a degree that we eventually get ready to sacrifice all that we are and all that we have for the service of the One Life.

There are twelve main obstacles to love and joy. If you conquer or avoid these obstacles, your love and joy will increase.

The first obstacle is pressure. Any time you exercise pressure on others, or try to force your will upon the will of others, love and joy weaken and eventually disappear. Love and joy increase only in a state of freedom.

People even try to use pressure with their thoughts, ideas, visions, dreams and art, but eventually they realize that a growing rejection is accumulating against them. True joy and love do not need pressure. Radiate your love, radiate your joy, radiate your beauty. Do not use any form of pressure. True friends and co-workers are those who come to you because of their free choice. Forced friendship eventually becomes a source of sorrow.

The second obstacle is jealousy. Jealousy saps the energy of love and joy. It burns the tissues of the etheric, astral and mental vehicles, and dissipates love and joy. Jealousy wants to possess, and whoever possesses anything eventually loses his love and his joy. He loses his life.

A jealous person acts as an unconscious agent for dark forces. Jealousy prevents growth of joy and love between people. It destroys the seeds of future accomplishments.

The third obstacle is the denial of freedom of other persons. Such a violation literally extinguishes the flame of your love and joy. Only in freedom does joy increase and love bloom. Let the one you love be free; in his or her freedom, find your own joy. Let that person decide or plan, follow his own conscience, and use his own free will. If you keep such an attitude, not only with your closest ones, but with all people, you will see the increase of love and joy in your heart.

Respect the ideas and the visions of others; be tolerant and make them respect your ideas and visions. If your ideas and visions are more inclusive, you will increase your love and joy.

The fourth obstacle to joy and love is the tendency to misuse people and their belongings. With such a tendency, love and joy eventually evaporate, because the spirit of exploitation rests in your heart.

There were two friends, a boy and a girl, who were in love and joyful. One day, the boy asked the girl, "How much do you make monthly?"

"Nine hundred dollars."

"You are really a darling. I love you so much! You know how much I love you, don't you?"

"Yes, I do."

"I want to go to school, and if you support me for five years, I will become a lawyer and then take care of you."

The girl hesitated, but because of her emotions she agreed, and they were married. They had two children before the boy graduated from law school. The girl did her best to support her husband. After he graduated, he came to me to speak about his graduation.

"How beautiful! You did it! And your wife was a heroine. For five years she supported you...."

"But," he said, "I would like to leave her."

"Leave her? For whom?"

"Just a divorce."

"But?..."

"I am falling in love with someone else."

"Really? What does your wife think?"

"I don't know. She is a little concerned."

"But for five years she supported you!"

"Yes, but...."

They were divorced, and he found the ways and means to pay minimum support for the children. Often he would come to my office and I would ask him, "Are you happy?"

"Sort of. I like this girl; we have great fun, but there is something in me that is closed. I can't love. I am not joyful, and she senses it...."

"You cannot manipulate or use people with love," I said, "because the fountain of love goes dry without sacrifice, sincerity and loyalty." I never saw him again.

The fifth obstacle is non-inclusiveness. Non-inclusiveness is a great enemy of love and joy. Love and joy are like fragrances; they expand and spread. Non-inclusiveness creates barriers and walls in your inner world.

Inclusiveness opens the path of expansion. Joy and love cannot be caged; they must flow and expand. Inclusiveness leads to right human relations, to international understanding, to respect, and to appreciation.

Non-inclusiveness is self-worship and separation, which eventually breeds aggressiveness, hatred and conflict. Joy and love disappear in an atmosphere of separation. Once they disappear, hatred and depression take their place.

The sixth obstacle is unrighteousness. If you are unrighteous in your thoughts, emotional responses and actions, you will not have real joy in your heart, and love will never bloom in you.

Joy and love increase when you respect the rights of other people. Those people who were not righteous to others carry a heavy burden in their conscience, and eventually that burden turns into a pressure and expresses itself through various sicknesses and complications in their lives.

A righteous person has joy and love, even if people do not understand him.

The seventh obstacle to joy and love is ugliness. Beauty increases joy and love; ugliness makes them disappear. Your love and joy fade away when you experience an ugly thought, emotion, action, or any ugly expression. Your thoughts are ugly when they are selfish, harmful, criminal, separative, false, and so on. Your emotions are ugly when they are negative, when they lack solemnity. Your actions and expressions are ugly when they are destructive, insulting, belittling, and motivated by self-interest.

As one removes ugliness from his surroundings, from his thoughts, emotional reactions and actions, joy fills his heart and love increases in him. Beauty always shines in joy and love.

The eighth obstacle is insincerity. No love or joy exists in a heart which has an insincere attitude toward other human beings. Love and joy cannot exist where sincerity is absent. An insincere person eventually finds his love and joy fading away. Insincerity causes disintegration in mental substance, and severs the thread between the Inner Guide and the person. To have joy and love, one must strive with all his heart to be sincere and honest with the world.

The ninth obstacle to joy and love is nosiness. A nosy person cannot increase his love and joy. He is always occupied with personality affairs. He criticizes and judges; he interferes with the decisions of others, mentally or verbally. He evokes reactions and involvement with the personal lives of others.

Love does not like nosiness. Joy does not live where there is imposition of thoughts and manners.

Nosiness increases your worries and hurts other people. A nosy person cannot gain his freedom; often he is caught in the net of gossip.

The tenth obstacle is criticism. Criticism creates rejection. Your aura hardens in its periphery. Every time you criticize, you impose yourself on others; you impose your personality on others. Your personality grows thick in such a way that your Soul hardly finds a chance to shine out.

Criticism does not let other people experience and experiment. It does not let them grow and be themselves. Criticism presents and imposes its own molds, and wants everyone to be molded by its standards. Thus, it limits the horizons and striving of others.

Love And Joy 143

Love and joy cannot grow and expand in an atmosphere of criticism. Love and joy exist for all. When you hurt someone, you hurt your love and your joy.

The eleventh obstacle to joy and love is carelessness and pride. The two go together. Love cares. Joy communicates and identifies with the souls of others, with the success and achievements of others.

Carelessness leads one to irresponsibility. Where the sense of responsibility does not exist, there is no conscious love and real joy. Love and joy are two great pillars of light which lead people toward spirituality, toward universality and toward the highest values of life. Love and joy cannot exist in an atmosphere polluted with human weaknesses and vices.

Pride is separative. Love is whole. Pride belittles others. Love and joy stand for the beauty and the interest of others.

People think that love and joy are personal properties. They are not personal properties. They are like sunshine, like air, like the fragrance of the hills. They belong to all, or they do not exist. Pride repels all joy and love.

The twelfth obstacle to love and joy is attachment. You attach to something or somebody and say, "I love her, him, or it." But eventually you will be surprised when you try to make it your property and own it for your own enjoyment, because you will slowly lose your love and joy.

Attachment to any love-object makes you lose your joy, and your love for that object will bring great disappointment. One cannot hold onto the object of his love and joy. Only through non-attachment to your love-object can you perpetuate your love and joy.

Love increases when you give love and let people love the way they want. You increase your joy by increasing the pure joy of others. You cannot run after love and joy; they are within you, and everywhere. In searching for love and joy, you lose yourself. In being love and joy, you find your True Self.

Joy and love create an element in our etheric body, and precipitate a kind of substance in our nerve channels which melts the poisons accumulated in our system through irritation, sorrow, depression and other negative emotions, thoughts or actions.

Lastly, joy and love expand the field of our magnetism within our aura, and we receive inspiration and impressions from Higher Realms, Galaxies, and Great Existences. Such a contact extremely enriches our creative abilities.

Those who live in the light of beauty, joy, love and freedom, live in the future and create a culture which will evoke the best creative powers from coming generations. This is how the path of perfection for humanity is paved toward greater achievement, and toward greater health and bliss.[9]

Indeed, in every striving to the summits, in every ascent, is contained an untold joy. An inner impulse irresistibly calls people towards the heights. [10]

---

[9] Taken from Chapter 11 in *The Flame of Beauty, Culture, Love, Joy,* by T. Saraydarian.

[10] Roerich, Nicholas K. *Himavat,* p. 12.

Index

Abstraction, moment of 7
Abundance 11,12
Abuse, sexual 32
Actions
    joyful 74
    ugly 141
Actualization, self-105,121
Admiration 43,44
Adultery 40
Affirmations 72
Aggressiveness 141
Agitation 34
Akbar 62
Alcohol 23
Alertness 18
Alignment 16-17
Anesthetics 80
Anger 28,34,49,69,97,102,118,132
Animosity 34
Anxiety 34
Apathy 132
Appreciation 141
Aquarius 52
Armageddon 132
Army, of Light 36
Art 128
Ashram 138
Aspiration 29,70,126
Asylums 61
At-one-ment 118
Ataturk 3
Atoms, permanent 32
Attachment 127,143
Attacks, psychic 42,129

Aura(s) 9,11,33,72,108,123,128,135, 142,144
    capsules of joy in 9
    crystallized joy in 81
    effect of admiration on 44
    friction in 45
    in ecstasy 40
    joy in 41
    joy locked in 19
Awareness, levels of 8
Awareness unit 16

Bailey, Alice 57
Balance 37-38
Battle 36
    joy in 90
    spiritual 57-58
Beads, on beam of light 24
Beam(s)
    of bliss 40
    of light 24
Beauty 8,15,34,35,105,121-122,141-142
    admiration for 43
    def. of 67
    role in increasing joy 43
    striving toward 62
Beings, angelic 33
Beingness 7-17, 39
Betrayal 131
Bhagavad Gita, quote from 115
Blessing, objects and money 77-78
Bliss 7,23,29,40,51,67,68,77,88,91,94, 95,99,109,117,119,144
    compared to joy 7

def of 8,14,110,118,122
is God 50
phases of 112
rel. to joy 36,45,54
rel. to joy and happiness 50-51
Blood 42,129
Bodilessness, joy of 45
Body(ies) 94,96
    astral 127
    chemistry in 11
    effect of joy on 128
    etheric 49,79-80,144
    mental 63
    sending joy to 76
    synchronization through joy 49
Brain 32
Buddha 62,95,112
Business, effect of joy in 53-54

Calmness, brought by admiration 44
Cancer, cause of 42
Capsules
    joy 27
    of joy in aura 9
Carelessness 143
Center(s) 33,105,127
    burning of 14
    effect of joy on 117
    emotional, stimulated by joy 49
    etheric 123
    heart 95,96
Ceremony
    admission to a brotherhood 36
    Armenian church 77
Chalice [see also Treasury] 16,89,91, 123
Challenge for Discipleship, excerpt from 93-108
Changeless One 15,101
Changelessness 14-15,91,101,102, 116
Child(ren) 11,20,31,44,61

Christ 41,62,76,95,105,113,137
    crucifixion of 67,77
    words of 50,59,63,64,116
Cleavages 13,69
Co-workers 36,104,108,117,139
Common Good 12,102
Compassion, def. of 98
Complaint 107
Condition adverse 100
Conflict, joy in 90
Confucius 62
Conscience 68
Consciousness 24,37,38,42,110, 123
    continuity of 33
    elevated by joy 53
    expanding 13
    expansion of 12,49,55,67,101,102, 105,106,128,130
    frozen 10
    regenerating 81
    Soul-c. 114,115,117,120
    unconditioned 7
    v. mind 12-13
Constellations, love and joy in 94
Contact
    created by joy 24
    of joy with body 63
    with Higher Worlds 33
    with joy 37
Contemplation 8
Contentment 98
Cooperation 34
Cooperativeness 18
Core 7,13,35,50
    Inner 37,62,63,113
    manifestation of 126
Corruption 36
Courage 90,104
Creativity 11,13,33,39,43,93,114,127, 135
    def. of 117

Crime(s) 11,29,94
  def. of 97
  karma of 103
  movies about 119-120
  of creating cleavages 14
Criminal(s) 35
  homes of 11
Criticism 44,142
Crucifixion 67,77

Dance 31
Daring 103,122
Death 110
Deception, self- 121
Depression 10,32,55,122,137,141,144
  cause of 42,52
  decisions under 49
Despair 32
Destruction 94
  spiritual 12
Detachment 7,37,55
Devotion 126
Digestion 107
Diligence 18
Discouragement 38,67
Discrimination 119
Disease(s) 38
  caused by resistance 45
  healing with joy 34
  of unhappiness 29
  sexually-transmissible 34
Doctor(s), using joy 50
Doubts 14,34,122
Drugs 23,24,29

Ecstasy 8,10,91,117,118,126
  def. of 40
  experiences of 54
  in sex 39-40
  of St. Stephen during stoning 51
Ego 34,68,97,106
Elder Brothers 38

Emanation(s), of joy 108
Emotion(s) 34,50,65,128,140-141,
Endlessness, joy of 37
Endurance 14, 107
Enemy(ies)
  created by imposition 11
  of joy 118-120
  respecting 131
Energy(ies)
  of joy 50
  psychic 42,75,78
  thought 42
Enlightenment 125
Enthusiasm 53,127
Essence 126
Evil 11,42
Evolution, through joy 42
Exaltation 133-134
Exercise(s) [see also visualization]
  for creating a new identity 47
  on joy 19-46
  re-experiencing a joy someone
    shared with you 27
  re-experiencing another's
    joy 26
  re-experiencing past joys 20
  remembering joyful
    experiences 81-82
  remembering joys others gave
    to you 28
  remembering joys received
    from Nature 28
  remembering joys you gave to
    others 28
Expansion
  of consciousness [see
    under consciousness]
  through joy 66
Eyes 18

Face 18
  effect of joy 58-59

148 *Index*

Faith, increases joy 70
Faithfulness 47
Family 32
Fanatic, def. of 111
Fanaticism 97,102
Fasting 32
Father
    in heaven 14,50
    of T.S.
        chasing butterfly 5-6
        story about 107
        story of empty pharmacy 2-5
Fear 25,34,69,111,122
    decisions under 49
    enemy of joy 101,118
    freedom from 29
Fearlessness 127
Fire(s)
    creative 11,97
    of joy 15
    of space 131
Food, assimilation of 129
Force(s)
    Creative 36
    dark 17,129,137,139
    of destruction 36
    of unity 13
Forgetfulness, self- 29
Forgiveness 98
Freedom 8,34,35,55,127,139
    denial of 139
    pursuit of 29
    Soul- 117
    through right thinking 121
Friends, true 139

Genocide 2
Gifts 74,105
Glamour(s) 127,135
Glands [see also under system] 49,58,85
    stimulated by joy 49

Gloom 67
God 24,35,52,68
    "G. is love" 130
    in human being 67
    is bliss 50
    kingdom of 31,64
    living 51
Goodness 8,11,34,35
    thought as factor of 42
Goodwill 120
Gossip 34,44,51,65,68
Gratitude 30,94,98
    characteristic of child 31
    releases joy 43
Great Ones 8,32,69,107-108,138
    joy of meeting 45
Greed 14,31,69,105
    def. of 60
    enemy of joy 118-119
Grief 10,49,52
Groups, integration of through joy 53
Guide, Inner [see also Self, Transpersonal; Soul; Watch, Inner] 120,142
Guilt 85,103
    def. of 67

Habit(s) 14,96
Hand, Guiding 38
Happiness 29,50,89,112
    cause of 63
    def. of 50,61
    effect on relationships 52
    rel. to bliss 50-51
    rel. to joy 45,54
    search for 109-112
Harmfulness 97
Harmlessness 29,70,88
Harmony 11,90
    in sound 12
    through love and joy 128

Hatred 11,28,34,69,97,131,132
   decisions made under 49
   def. of 119
   devours joy 44
   enemy of joy 119
Healers, spiritual 41
Healing 9,125
   through joy 29,34,49,50,51,79, 105
   through love and joy 128
   with joy and wormwood oil 38
Health 18,57,99,144
   brought by admiration 44
   mental 128
   of spirit 137
Heart 11,13
   effect of joy on 39
   frozen 10
   joy of 54
   manifested in joy 106
   strengthening 129
Hercules 95
Hero(es) 38
   ecstasy of 51
Heroism 36
Hierarchy 114-117,137
Hilarity, vs. joy 29
Home, path to 45
Hospitals, use of joy in 39
Hosts, angelic 108
Humility, when building spiritual identity 47
Hypocrisy 25,34,69

Identification, with problems 9
Identity, exercise for creating new 47
Ignorance 36
Illusions 135
Imagination, creative 27-28
Immortality 101
   conscious 95
   def. of 114
Imperil 38
Inclusiveness 70,98,128
   non- 140-141
Inertia 132
Infinity 37,91,118,134
Ingratitude 131
Initiate 39
Insincerity 141-142
Inspiration 11,90,107
Integration 16
Interest, self- 14,16,131
Intuition 128
Invulnerability 115
Irritation 14,34,38,75,144

Jealousy 14,34,69,97,132,139
Joy [see also Exercises] 29,30,31,36, 37,39,45,49,52,53-54,55,76-77,102,111,114,130,138
   and love 93-108,127-131
   blocked 9-10
   builds continuity of consciousness 33
   capsules in aura 9
   combined with love 39-40
   compared to bliss 7-8
   conditions necessary to release 101-105
   decisions made in 49
   def. of 2,7,11,12,13,14,16,17,18, 22,23,24,28,34,45,50,51,65, 66,75,89,90,91,115,116,119, 120,122-123,133-134,137
   developed by admiration 43
   enemies of 118-120
   exercises on 19-47
   frozen 10
   healing power of 38
   healing through 50,51
   how to increase 96-100
   in group integration 53-54

in labor 133
in training leaders 29
observation of 8,9
obstacles to 139-144
of timelessness 37-38
psychology of 30-31
rel. to abundance 12
rel. to bliss 36,50-51
rel. to endurance 14
rel. to irritation 38
rel. to magnetism 76
rel. to memory 32
rel. to patience 14
rel. to perseverance 14
rel. to psychic energy 42
rel. to righteousness 15-16
released by gratitude 43
seven qualities of 65-67
used with wormwood oil 38
v. bliss, happiness 45
v. hilarity 29
ways to help people remember 45-46
ways to lose 34
"Joy is a special wisdom" 29,33,35, 56,88,89
Joylessness 11

Karma 103,119
Kingdom(s) 13
of God 31,64
Krishna 62

Labor 9,11,13,16,37,104,108,122
creative 103
def. of 133
enthusiasm in 11
joy in 37
rel. to joy and love 96,97,98
Lao Tsu 62
Law(s) 29
of Change 116-117

of Love 116
of reaping what you sow 35
Laziness 100
Leader(s) 8,29,51
Letters
writing 105
written in joy 75
Lies, enemy of joy 120
Light 35,36,63
in Subtle World 43
of joy 52
rel. to joy 125
Lives, past 16,34
Loneliness 13,42,104,110
Lotus 89,123
Love 7,11,29,119
and joy 93-108
combined with joy 39
def. of 114
how to increase 96-99
level of 130,131-132
meaning of "to love" 100
obstacles to 139-144
permanent 138
rel. to joy 7
Lovingness 18
Loyalty 141
Lying 52

M.M. [see under Master]
Magnanimity, def. of 133
Magnetism 76,89,90,107,128,144
Malice 34,44,97
Marijuana 23
Martyrs 14
story of St. Stephen 51
Master(s) 94
D.K. 67
M.M. 37, 39,75
Meditation 8,117-118
on joy 87
on virtues 120

scientific 120-121
to increase love and joy 99
when to avoid 66
Mediums 77
Memory(ies)
from Chalice 16
of Home 109
painful 32
rel. to joy 32
releasing m. of joy 27
Mind
conscious 16
v. consciousness 13
Miracle(s)
in life 43
of joy 7,28
through joy 39,58
Monad 24
Money, blessing 78
Movies, criminal 32
Murder 32

Nature 28,29,30,43,44,55,61
Negativity 61,106
Nerve(s) 10,129
channels 144
Nirvana, def. of 45
Nobility 11
Nosiness, obstacle to love
and joy 142

Object(s)
charge on 42
charging with joy 76
of admiration 43-44
Observation(s) 9
about joy 18
of effects of joy 9
of joy 1,22,54
Obstacles
to joy 32
to love and joy 139-144

Oneness 14
Openness 18
Organ(s), sending joy to 79

Paralysis, cured by joy exercises
40-41
Past, comparing with present 21
Patience 14
Peace, 34,44,70,88
def. of 63
Perfection 43,88
Permanency, source of joy 101
Perseverance 14
Personality 112,128
Physicians 25
Pity, self- 108
Plan 114,115,117,130
Plans, joyful 72-73
Plane(s) 7,125-126
Intuitional 40
mental 39,110-111
Pollution 69
Prana 107,128
Prejudice(s) 14,49
Pressure, obstacle to love and
joy 139
Pretension 34,68
Pride 143
Prisoners, homes of 11
Prisons 61
Problems, solving with joy 30,74
Programming 30-31
Promotion 29
Psychiatrists 19,21,25,44
Psychologist(s) 2,10,19,31
Psychology, of joy 30-31
Punctuality 18
Punishment, v. exercises of joy 29
Purification 65,106
Purity 103
Purpose 36,130
Divine 51

Index

Questioning, step toward joy 121

Radiance 18
Rapture, def. of 45,54
Regeneration 65
Reincarnation 35
Relations, right human 141
Relationship(s), right 53,74
Religion 29,69
Remorse 28
Respect 141
Responsibility, sense of 15,100, 104,143
Resurrection 67
Revelation 127
Revenge 34,44,69,97
Righteousness 8,34,35,70
    sense of 15

Sacrifice 35,89,105,131,141
Sadness 10,31
Saint John, words of 51
Saint Stephen, story of stoning 51
Saintliness 103
Samadhi 8,51
Satan 52
Schools, joy in 53
Science, of joy 34
Scientists 132
Secretion(s), effect of joy on 39
Self 23,36,51,62,84,101,109,133,
    All- 96
    Essential Self 126
    One 14
    Transpersonal 114,120
    True 7,8,9,62138,143
Sense(s)
    buried 12
    effect of joy on 39

    five 126
    of responsibility 15
    of righteousness 15
    of unity 7
Sensitiveness 18
Sensitivity, magnetic 41
Separation 141
Separatism 13,34,68,97
Separativeness 9,137
Serenity 89
Service 15,29,34,35,89,102,103,126
    def. of 114,115
    greater field 104
    increases joy 60,62
    sacrificial 9,36,96
    to Hierarchy 138
Sex 29,39-40,54-66
Sharing, of joy 106-107
Shield, of joy 17,36,37,129
Sickness(es)
    cause of 135
    through lack of joy 57
Simplicity 70,90
Sincerity 70,141
Slander 34,44,52,97
Slavery 36
Sleep 34
Smile 25,136-137
Solemnity 47,133
Songs, during joy 108
Sorrow 32,77,137-144
Soul(s) [see also Guide, Inner; Self, Transpersonal; Watch, Inner]
    8,11,49,51,93,96,99,113,114, 116,122,123,142
    -awareness 114
    -consciousness 114-115,117,120
    -infusion 120
    human 8,16,94,95,137

Index 153

rhythm of 12
Space 27,134-137
   fire of 131
Spacelessness 15
Spark 50,109,117
Speech 29
Spiritual Triad 7,8,95,96,117,118,119
Stars 37
Story of:
   Ataturk meeting father of T.S. 3-4
   black shepherds (joy) 56-57
   boy passing exams after imagining joy 57-58
   boy who became lawyer and left his wife 140
   boy who could not find joy in life 23
   chasing butterfly 5-6
   child who fed dog his dinner (joy) 30
   depressed boy healed by joy 54-55
   father solving problems with joy 53-54
   fever cured by joy 57
   giving bad news before lecture 66
   heart surgeon close to death 111
   heart surgeon who developed joy 25
   holy man in meditation (ecstasy) 117-118
   jade from medium 77
   man cured of paralysis through joy exercises 40
   pharmacy 2-5
   postal worker who learned to smile 136-137
   producer of criminal movies 119-120
   sergeant chosen for his joy 56
   sister of T.S. sharing her ball in joy 106
   T.S. seeing dances without sisters (joy, shares) 107
   teacher shot by arrow 8
   teacher whose watch disappeared 115
   ugly toy 119
   violinist who quit playing (lost joy) 59
   visiting old-age home (teaching joy) 31
   wife who saved her marriage with just a few dollars (show love and joy) 73-74
   wife who wanted servant 60
   woman who lost her beauty 112-113
Strength 99
Striving 7,11,35,43,62,126
Students, using joy exercises with 28
Study, when to avoid 66
Sublimation 106,127
Success 11
   def. of 90
   rel. to magnetism 76
   through joy 54,55,56,75
   visualizing 84
Suffering 112
Suggestions, post-hypnotic 32
Suicide 69,94
Superstitions 14
   eliminated by joy 49
Surgery 58
   etheric 79-80
Survival, potentials 11
Sweat, of joy 85
Symphony, Cosmic 94
Synthesis 13,34,62-63
System(s)
   endocrine 39

glandular 39,49
immune 12

Talents, from Chalice 16
Teaching 35,64,65
    of joy 7
    with joy 11
Tears, chemistry of 85
Temple, of God 51
The Science of Becoming Oneself,
    excerpt from 89-91
Thinking 13,18,43,120
Thought(s) 29,42
    harmful 96
    joyful 71-72
    seed t. on joy 88
    ugly 141
Timelessness 15,37-38
Totalitarianism 30,36
Tranquility 70
Transfiguration 18,45
Transformation 10,14,18,33,41,45,94
Transmutation 18,45
Treason 32,34,52
Treasury [see also Chalice] 16,22,32
Truth 120
Tyrant 15

Ugliness 119-120,141
Unfoldment, through joy 67
Unhappiness 12,29,30
United Nations 127
Unity 7,13,29
Universality 142-143
Unrighteousness 34,141
Upanishads 36
    excerpt from 109
Upliftment 9

Values, distortion of 37
Vanity(ies) 14,34,68
Vices 23,24

Victory 57,62
Vigor 89
Violence 132
Virtues, meditation on 120
Vision 90
Visualization [see also exercises]
    to cure paralysis 40
    to increase love and joy 98-99
Vitality 11-12,18,135

Want, freedom from 29
War, atomic 132
Warriors
    of life 7
    salutation 91
Watch, Inner [see also Guide, Inner;
    Self, Transpersonal; Soul]
    8,105
Watchman 17
Will 97,127
    Divine 36,95
    imposition of 11
    power 125
Wisdom 16,35,36
Withdrawal, to higher level 8
World(s)
    Fiery 134,138
    Higher 33,37,41,43,45,69,128
    Other 45
    Subtle 43,134,138
Wormwood oil 38

Zoroaster 95